Friday Morning Reflections at the World Bank

Friday Morning Reflections at the World Bank

Essays on Values and Development

David Beckmann

Ramgopal Agarwala

Sven Burmester

Ismail Serageldin

Foreword by

Barber B. Conable

Seven Locks Press
Washington

Manufactured in the United States of America
Cover illustration by Engeman's Dream Works, Washington, DC
Typesetting by Edington-Rand, Inc., Riverdale, MD
Printed by McNaughton & Gunn, Inc., Saline, MI

Seven Locks Press is a Washington-based book publisher of non-fiction works on social, political, and cultural issues. It takes its name from a series of lift locks on the Chesapeake and Ohio Canal.

For more information or a catalog:

Seven Locks Press
P.O. Box 27
Cabin John, MD 20818
(301) 320-2130

Contents

Foreword

On Friday mornings at the World Bank, a concerned and involved group of people meet to discuss, from their own unique viewpoints, the moral values involved in their work. Almost every religion is represented, and every continent. These discussions have been a satisfying experience for this group, and from them this book has been written.

The World Bank is not a bank, but a development institution; its goal not orderly and profitable finance, but the reduction of the scourge of poverty. It is a large bureaucracy, deliberately incorporating the experience, skills and motivations of people from all over the world. More than 45 years after its founding, the World Bank's central development role is accepted, its resources large, and its credibility unquestioned. New development-related initiatives, whether generated internally or externally, tend to gravitate into its program because the Bank is the only institution equipped to handle them. Debt problems, environmental concerns, the restructuring of socialist societies, oil shocks, global recession—to these and similar future developments the World Bank is expected, quite properly, to respond.

Is the World Bank successful? Poverty persists, compounded by faulty governance, population growth, widespread illiteracy, obstacles to trade and the uneven distribution of resources. Success and failure, in development, have many components; but without the tremendous cooperative effort the World Bank represents, the upward slope would be much steeper.

Preface

True development is not measured by macroeconomic statistics, but by real improvement in the quality of life of individual people. In the same sense, development is not an impersonal force, so much as a triumph of individual effort enhanced by cooperation. Skillful, highly-motivated people support and lift each other by common understanding and encouragement. Happily, development is not one of those human concerns about which people easily disagree, particularly now that East-West tensions seem to be declining.

This book is about the exploration of common values. Family members can take each other's values for granted, but people from opposite sides of the world need the reassurance of community. To make a lifetime of commitment to a process or an institution requires a certain amount of exploration and introspection. It is not enough to have a secure job: one must be satisfied with one's colleagues and one's own motivations. There is no strength in diversity without the cement of commonly-held values.

The writers of this book have consciously explored their community of values along the avenue of their common purpose. Readers of this book should find reassurance about humanity's future in what has been written here. These very different authors are bound together by a common moral fiber, no matter what label identifies their origin or their religious upbringing. That is what humanity is all about.

Barber B. Conable
President, The World Bank

Preface

David Beckmann

Every Friday morning at 8 o'clock about 25 people gather for coffee and discussion about the role of values at the World Bank and, more generally, in the world's development.

The group's members are nearly all Bank staff, including both secretaries and vice presidents. Women and men from all over the world, they represent a variety of religious and cultural traditions. The composition of the group varies from week to week, but it might well include a Catholic from Cameroon, a Jew from the United States, a Palestinian, an evangelical Protestant from Australia, several Hindus, and some who distrust all religion. Most Bank staff travel, and on any Friday morning someone might just have returned from Somalia, another from Indonesia, and another from Brazil.

The World Bank is the world's largest official institution for the promotion of international development. It invests in projects and encourages policies designed to foster economic growth and reduce poverty in developing countries. Our Friday group is united in finding that our work pushes us, on a daily basis, to relate morality, ethics, and religion to the large investments and economic policy questions the Bank faces.

We take turns leading the discussion. One customary format is for a group member to speak briefly about his or her life experience and the values that have shaped it. Then the speaker suggests the implications of those values for the work of the Bank and for development generally. Group discussion ensues and often continues the next week.

A Korean woman tells of her childhood in poverty when she helped her mother sell baked potatoes on the side of the road. She recounts several of the wise and beautiful stories her mother told her during those years.

A man from Lesotho relates his experience of close community in his home village and explores its relevance to his present work as a manager in a large, international bureaucracy.

A U.S. woman shares her unusually vivid experiences in prayer and the strong sense of mission she now brings to her work.

An official from the People's Republic of China, a visitor to the Bank, discusses Chinese attitudes toward development, economic liberalization, and nuclear war. He shares the conflict between his modern values and his father's insistence on traditional patterns of family behavior.

Sometimes senior officials of the Bank speak to the group from an explicitly ethical perspective. The Bank's last three presidents — Robert McNamara, A.W. Clausen, and Barber B. Conable — have all met with the group. Guest speakers from outside the Bank have included Dom Helder Camara, the elder statesman of liberation theology in Latin America; A.T. Ariyaratne, founder of a Buddhist social development movement that now includes 8,000 villages in Sri Lanka; Johannes Witteveen, formerly Managing Director of the International Monetary Fund and a Sufi master; M. Scott Peck, a writer on psychology and spirituality; and Fritzjov Kapra, the philosopher of physics.

The group has repeatedly discussed how the Bank can be more effective in reducing poverty and protecting nature. It has reflected on global trends, such as liberalization among the Communist countries. And its members have read and discussed such books as E.F. Schumacher's *Guide for the Perplexed*, Robert M. Pirsig's *Zen and the Art of Motorcycle Maintenance*, and Joseph Campbell's *Myths to Live By*.

We have listened with appreciation and sometimes wonder to varied autobiographies, beliefs, and professional concerns. We have learned from one another, and our minds have been opened to each other's ideas. Our generalizations about other cultures and religions have been moderated, and we have gained clarity in our own beliefs as we have tried to explain them to people who do not share them. We have modified our views on economic and political issues in trying to relate these issues to our most basic beliefs.

The Friday morning group began when a few of us agreed to meet for six weeks to share our convictions about values and development. The discussion has gone on for more than a decade. Others have joined, some for a few weeks and some for a period of years.

The authors of this volume have been shaped by four different traditions — Hindu, Christian, humanist, and Muslim. But our various traditions have led us to a common conclusion: that spiritual values have been dangerously slighted in shaping the world's development and that humanity's survival may be at stake.

We are publishing the book for two reasons. First, we hope that the combined witness of four traditions may encourage others in their efforts to insert ethical considerations into economics and politics.

Second, we believe that the practical application of ethics in our pluralistic world depends on sensitivity to creeds other than our own. We hope this book will demonstrate how fruitful it is for persons from different backgrounds to discuss world problems in the context of ethical and religious values.

Such discussion has made us more aware of how much religious and ethical traditions have in common. Each of the world's traditions is grappling with the problems and possibilities that confront the world as a whole in our century, and we have found this matter-of-fact unity a fruitful starting point for reconsideration of long-standing religious and philosophical issues.

A few words about each of us. Ramgopal Agarwala has played a lead role in preparing several major World Bank reports on Africa over the last decade, most recently *Sub-Saharan Africa: From Crisis to Sustainable Growth* (1989). He was formerly responsible for structural adjustment lending to Korea and before that served in the Bank's resident mission in Bangladesh. He did his undergraduate studies in India and holds a doctorate in economics from Manchester, England. He is author of *An Econometric Model for India* (Frank Cass 1970) and has contributed many articles to professional journals.

David Beckmann is senior advisor at the World Bank on nongovernmental organizations. He leads a team that has guided a major expansion of World Bank involvement with grassroots groups and other nongovernmental organizations. He previously worked as a speechwriter for the Bank's president and before that was a project officer for low-cost housing and slum improvement projects in East Africa and Latin America. He is a Lutheran pastor and worked for a Lutheran-supported development program in Bangladesh before coming to the Bank. His books include *The Overseas List: Opportunities for Living and Working in the Developing Countries* (Augsburg 1985). In 1991, he was elected president of Bread for the World, the Christian citizen's movement to reduce hunger, and is leaving the World Bank to assume this new responsibility.

Sven Burmester is deputy secretary of the Bank. In that capacity, he deals with the Board of Executive Directors, which represents member countries. He was previously in charge of lending for education in countries along the Pacific rim of Asia, including the People's Republic of China. He also served as division chief for the Horn of Africa and as personal assistant to Robert McNamara when he was president of the Bank. Sven Burmester holds graduate degrees in chemistry and public affairs and was adjunct professor at Georgetown University from 1980 to 1988. He speaks ten languages and is well known in Denmark as a newspaper columnist, television commentator, and author. His latest book is *USA: Land of the Middle Class* (in Danish).

Ismail Serageldin is director of the Technical Department of the Africa Regional Office. He was formerly director of the Bank's programs in nine West African countries. He had previously served as division chief for urban development projects in the Middle East and North Africa and, before that, as chief of a division that provides technical assistance on a paid basis to high-income countries in the Middle East. His most recent books are *Poverty, Adjustment, and Growth in Africa* (World Bank 1989) and *Space for Freedom: The Search for Architectural Excellence in Muslim Society* (Butterworth 1989).

We are very much indebted to Harriet Baldwin, another long-term member of the Friday group. She gave us extensive editorial assistance, shaping our separate essays into a readable whole. She interested Seven Locks Press.

The essays in this book express our own personal beliefs. They touch on many issues outside the official purview of the World Bank. Clearly, the Bank is not responsible for, and does not necessarily deal with, the thoughts expressed here.

We begin each Friday morning with a moment of silence. Some of us pray, some meditate, and some just relax and remember that life is more than chatter and activity. This quiet time together is an important part of our discussion, and so we invite the reader to pause and share a moment of reflective silence.

A Harmonist Manifesto: Hindu Philosophy in Action

Ramgopal Agarwala

My world view has been shaped primarily by four influences: Hinduism, Mahatma Gandhi, economics, and East Asia.

I grew up in an orthodox Hindu atmosphere and imbibed the philosophical base of Hinduism, whose key elements I understood to be the following. Spiritual truth is the most fundamental truth in life, and it can be experienced only through fervent search. The seers who experience this truth realize that human beings are potentially divine and that contact with that divinity gives the deepest and longest-lasting joy. Moreover, spiritual truth is one, although different sages state it differently, and persons endowed with different qualities search for it in different ways. Finally, satisfaction in life lies in doing one's duty and in moving toward realization of the potential divinity in us. Each one doing his duty best promotes the general welfare.

During my student days, I came to know of Gandhi, who brought spiritual principles to bear on the political struggle for freedom in India. He showed that spiritual life need not be detached from political and economic life and that spiritual truths can be tools for successful struggle in these arenas. At the same time, the tools must be adapted to fit the time and circumstances in order to be used successfully.

The third important influence in my life was economics, particularly Adam Smith's vision of the "invisible hand". I found it illuminating that there is an underlying harmony of interests of individuals in the economic sphere of society, provided that free markets are allowed to operate unhindered by vested interests, either of the government or of special interest groups. The free market operates as an "invisible hand" would write. The state may have to intervene at times to address equity problems (as Marx argued) and certain problems of macro-economic demand management (as Keynes argued). In addition, the issues of resource depletion and intergenerational equity have become increasingly important qualifications to the logic of the invisible hand. But the basic vision of harmony propounded by Adam Smith remains powerful; "Marketism" outlines a harmony in economics which is parallel to that which Hinduism discerns in the spiritual sphere.

The fourth and latest influence in my life is my work in East Asia, particularly Korea and Japan. In working and traveling in these countries, I have been struck by the importance they attach to balance and harmony. Nothing in life is all good or all bad: even a good thing carried to excess can be damaging. The important thing is to look for the balance appropriate to the circumstances where, in the language of economics, the marginal productivity of "good" things becomes equal to the marginal productivity of "bad" things. This East Asian approach leads to less than clear-cut answers to many social and political issues, but it is exceptionally conducive to social harmony.

Together these experiences have given me a world view that combines 1) the spiritual truth perceived by Hindus applied practically to contemporary problems, 2) the economic philosophy of Europeans, and 3) the social values of East Asia.

Mid-Century Hope to Late-Century Disillusionment

In the mid-1950s, when I was attending college in Calcutta, a heady atmosphere of optimism about the future prevailed. India, like many other ex-colonies, was launching its program for modernization: there was tremendous enthusiasm about science and technology, about economic development plans, and about democracy. Within a few decades the developing countries were expected to achieve economic "take-off" and reduce the "gap" that separated them from the developed countries. The developed countries, too, were experiencing an economic boom, partially fueled by the cold war, and assisted by a burst of technological developments and by cheap and abundant energy. It appeared that the developed countries could experience sustained growth and provide adequate welfare to the needy at home as well as assistance to poor countries abroad. The vista was one of limitless progress — progress in science, technology and human welfare.

However, within just one generation the mood has drastically changed. Today we often think of technology as a genie out of the bottle — out of human control. In developed countries, economists are perplexed by tenacious economic problems, think tanks suggest the possibility of reaching limits to growth, and politicians have been dismantling welfare systems built up over decades. In most of the developing countries, the hope of catching up with the developed countries in the foreseeable future has vanished. The battle against poverty seems likely to last for generations, if not centuries. With expectations raised and hopes of fulfilling them receding, the incidence of corruption and oppression among the powerful is increasing, as are hopelessness, desperation, and terrorism on the part of the disadvantaged.

This swift and dramatic turn of mood is profoundly ironic. It would be tragic if, in the wake of tremendous progress in science and technology and of liberating political developments, this century should end on such a fearsome note. The fact is that the world's productive potential today is higher than ever before. There are fewer deaths from starvation or famine than in any previous century. A child born today can be expected to live longer and be healthier than ever before. Improved communications have made the world a truly global village. By historical comparison, there is considerably increased interest in, knowledge of, and even tolerance of each other's culture. Most ethnic and religious minorities are now better protected. In most countries, the position of women — one half of humanity — is slowly improving. Even after rapid exploitation of resources, gross world wealth (that is, the total means of production, including known natural resources and physical and human capital) is probably higher today than ever before. In spite of the ever-present danger of nuclear war, the past three decades witnessed fewer deaths from wars than the three decades that preceded them. So why this pessimism? Why this disillusionment?

Our problems today are due more to a crisis of values than a crisis of energy or matter. The present darkness is like darkness before the dawn. Mankind is getting ready for a giant step forward, in the process of evolution, when the science and technology of the present will be fused with the spiritual insights of the past. Taking this step will require much hard work and hard thinking; but given the spiritual urge of human beings, I have confidence that such effort will be forthcoming. The present is a time for hope, excitement, and effort, not for anger, despair, or fear.

But the future can be properly shaped only if we have a clear-sighted view of the present problems. And the problems of the modern era are real and fundamental — real in that they are not due mainly to misconception, and fundamental in that they originate from the very roots of the modern system of values. The developed countries are suffering from excessive affluence, or what may be called the miseries of over-consumption. This is obvious in the case of food consumption: overeating is a serious problem in these countries that leads to obesity, undernourishment, and a variety of chronic diseases. Accumulating consumer durables takes so much time that there is no time for enjoying the appliances and gadgets; frantic efforts to "enjoy" them all result in little enjoyment from any of them. The relentless pursuit of material progress has resulted in a loss of joy in work and a loosening of family ties — with spouses, children, and parents. At the same time, boredom is leading to sexual promiscuity, drugs, and violence. Without basic redirection, these tendencies will lead to demoralization and ultimately threaten material prosperity itself.

At the same time, the developing countries are suffering from the miseries of poverty, compounded by the failure to meet rising expectations. Hunger and infant mortality are still widespread. Increased life expectancy has contributed to a worsening of the population problem; particularly in urban areas, overcrowding stifles human decency and dignity. The symbols of modernization — such consumer durables as television and cars — are visible to everybody; but for most of the population, they remain far out of reach. For the poor, this creates frustration and anger and encourages terrorism and anarchy. For the middle class, it is an invitation to corruption and oppression. Unless there is fundamental change, these tendencies will make it impossible for many developing countries to achieve, within the foreseeable future, even the elementary goals of meeting basic needs, not to speak of achieving more equitable distribution of wealth and democratic political institutions.

In addition, developed and developing countries share three dangers resulting directly from modernization — nuclear holocaust, resource depletion, and climactic changes. Unlike earlier wars, wars today can occur suddenly, within a matter of hours, and, if they involved nuclear weapons, could be totally devastating. Similarly, as shown already by the experience of artificially-induced oil shortages, resource depletion may bring about rapid and serious disruption on a scale not experienced before. Precisely because of their suddenness and decisiveness, these dangers have to be anticipated and prevented. Once they occur, it is too late to respond. Global warming due to the emission of gases from automobiles and other items of modern life is a slow process, but it could be devastating in terms of its impact on sea levels and climactic changes. Is it worth risking these dangers for the sake of ever-increasing material consumption, especially now that increasing consumption is producing so little additional happiness in the developed countries?

The root of the malaise in the modern world is a view that assumes conflict and struggle are at the center of life. This view has been enshrined in the biological theory of evolution, in the Marxian view of historical evolution, and in the modern global system of competition among nations. European civilization has thrived on this view, but technological developments now make it too risky for mankind.

The biological theory of evolution is consistent with biological facts. However, these facts do not necessarily support the interpretations of some evolution theorists — an interpretation enshrined in popular imagination — that nature is in conflict and at war within itself, engaged in a struggle to survive. This view might explain why evolution leads to biologically stronger creatures, but it does not explain why the process leads to creatures that are also intellectually and spiritually superior. The need for survival does not explain why the single cell amoeba evolves into more complex and vulnerable creatures.

The conflict theory of evolution has had far-reaching effects in social, economic, and political relations; it has encouraged conflicts among individuals and groups and the reckless exploitation of nature. The very fact that the yearning for peace is widespread among humanity suggests the need for re-examining the conflict-based interpretation of evolution.

A Spiritual Theory of Evolution

In order to come out of the present crisis, we need richer goals than materialism and better tools than rationalism.

We need to turn inward for both fulfillment and enlightenment.

Science and technology are powerful machines, but they need steering wheels to guide them. The religious and spiritual values of mankind can provide help in building such steering wheels. In going back to religions, one has to beware of the bigotry, oppression, and violence wrought in the name of religions. To avoid these pitfalls, spiritual insights and values derived from religions must go beyond classical rationalism without contradicting reason and science. In other words, a science of the spirit is needed to complement the science of matter.

Such a fusion between classical science and classical religion can only emerge over time. While no one can foresee the specifics of such fusion, it is worthwhile to examine a spiritual theory of evolution. Such a theory suggests that evolution is not random or without purpose, but is guided by the spirit that underlies everything in the world. This spirit is *potentially* divine — omnipotent and omniscient when fully manifest, but still struggling to make itself felt. Mankind is the most advanced form of this manifestation, but evolution is still an incomplete story.

The theory — which holds that the essential purpose of evolution is the manifestation of the underlying spirituality of all living creatures — is not scientific; it results from a leap of intuition. Nor is there any method of directly testing it. However, it is consistent with the facts of science and seems to answer many otherwise puzzling questions. For instance, the process of evolution appears to be systematic, but the more evolved species are not biologically stronger; rather, the consistent pattern of evolutionary growth seems to relate to spiritual consciousness. The existence of potential divinity or super-consciousness is indicated by our own experiences at moments of love and of creativity in science and art. It is also indicated by the religious prophets, who represent explosions of spiritual energy similar to nuclear explosions of material energy.

This divinity is only potential; the spirit is still struggling to be fully manifest in human lives. No all-powerful and all-merciful God takes care of all of our miseries, yet life is not just misery. If it were, why not kill oneself and/or others? Life is the medium through which the spirit is achieving fuller and fuller manifestation. That is the noble purpose of life; that is why killing any life is a sin, except when killing somehow assists the overall process of evolution.

As individuals internalize the underlying spirituality of all of life, it opens the springs of love and beauty within. Love thy neighbor as thyself, because deep down thy neighbor *is* thyself. This view gives deeper meaning to the principles of equality and liberty. Different human beings are equal just as different parts of the body are equal — head and heart are different but equally important. Each part must have the liberty to perform its appointed function, but not by interfering with the function of others. An awareness of shared divinity helps overcome the sense of loneliness and strengthens ties of family and group.

My belief in spiritual evolution leads me to an attitude toward life that I call "harmonism." Harmonism comprises three fundamental principles. First, we are all part of the same spirit. Second, deep down, we all share the objective of assisting the onward march of the spirit toward truth, love, and beauty. Third, we experience happiness to the extent we contribute to this common objective.

There is a fundamental harmony of interest among all living things in the world. The conflicts between humanity and nature, between man and woman, between nation and nation, and between labor and capital, are all superficial. This is not to underestimate the importance of conflict or the power of evil. We are often in conflict with ourselves because of our own ignorance and evil tendencies; we are also in conflict with others because of our own or others' ignorance and evil tendencies. We should bring the same love and understanding to struggles against others that we do to the struggle within ourselves. We should not idolize conflict as the law of life, for it leads not to life, but to death.

Harmonism provides an antidote to the present world crisis in the midst of plenty. It leads to a "needs-based" approach in place of a "wants-based" approach. A needs-based approach would help in slowing down the pace of depletion of natural resources in the developed countries and in checking the growth of consumption and oppression in developing countries.

Science and technology have done their job; properly utilized, they can fulfill all the material needs of human beings. The standard of living in the United States — roughly $20,000 per capita — could, even with improved efficiency, probably be sustained for only about one billion people. But with a needs-based standard, an income of $2,000 per capita would be adequate, and the world's resources could sustain about 10 billion people at that level of income indefinitely. With material needs taken care of, mankind could get on with its job of spiritual development. Eventually, human society will have to live by a needs-based approach. We could save ourselves much time and waste by coming to voluntary recognition of this before widespread resource depletion and conflict inevitably force it upon us.

Just as economics is the study of the material well-being of societies, harmonics is the study of the spiritual well-being of society. In economics, we deal with trade-offs, zero-sum games, and interpersonal and intergenerational exchanges. In this context, if I give away something I have less of it for myself; if I use a resource today, I have less of it for tomorrow. But for some resources — namely knowledge, love, and beauty — an exactly opposite law applies: the more I give the more I have, the more the resource is used the greater it becomes. Unlike physical resources, knowledge is not depleted by its use; it grows by use. If I give my knowledge to others, I don't have less of it; in fact, it gets clearer in my mind. Similarly, there is no limit to the amount of love available. If I give love to others, I don't have any less left for me; but simply get more. The boundary of love can be extended wider and wider without loss to those in inner circles. And a thing of beauty — a beautiful sunset, a beautiful poem, a beautiful painting — can be a source of joy to one without any loss to others.

Human civilization scaled new heights after the Renaissance in Europe when the harmonist view was applied to knowledge; then knowledge was not kept the secret preserve of the few but began to be shared and applied widely. Knowledge snowballed and grew. A similar view needs to be taken of love and beauty. Human civilization will take a new stride when mankind concentrates on widening its circle of love to include other human beings and nature around them.

A society based on harmonism will be more than just a "sustainable society." There have been many primitive societies which were sustainable. Instead, it will be a sustainable society with a cutting edge of spiritual advancement that will provide the excitement that has been so painfully lacking in recent years. Spiritual advancement is the antidote to the boredom that lies just below the surface of many of the ills of the modern world.

Harmonism and Development

What can be done to translate the harmonist paradigm into action? More specifically, what have I been doing to assist the process?

What is needed is an intellectual revolution: a switch from the conflict view of life to the harmonist view of life that calls for increased attention to inner sources of joy and increased appreciation of the inner voice within us all. This intellectual revolution can be achieved only over a long period through discussion among thoughtful people everywhere. It is most encouraging that there has been a steady stream of literature on the relation between science and spirituality, especially in the United States, where the fusion between science and religion may gradually occur.

These changes will take a long time, if they are to occur

at all. The immediate need is to debate these issues in a free and frank manner, in universities and elsewhere. The Friday morning group at the World Bank is an example of what can be done in many places. Debates and discussions will, over time, define the new paradigm, and action will follow ideas.

But action can begin at once. Several aspects of the World Bank's mission are in congruence with the new paradigm the world needs.

First, the idea of interdependence. Harmonist philosophy puts emphasis on interdependence rather than independence. The World Bank's approach is that development is in everybody's interest: growth in developing countries helps growth in the developed countries and *vice versa.*

Second, the importance of human needs. Since the mid-1970s, the World Bank has taken special steps to meet the basic needs of the poorest people in developing countries. This effort is in line with harmonist philosophy because of the spiritual potential of humanity. Throughout my years in the Bank, I have been involved with promoting policies and investment programs that contribute to meeting basic needs of the poor — not just the wants of the top few. Eliminating hunger, reducing infant mortality, promoting health, education, research, and technology — these are the day-to-day concerns that give a missionary zeal to working for the World Bank, especially in my recent assignments dealing with sub-Saharan Africa, where human needs are so great.

Third, the emphasis on "duties" more than on "rights," particularly at a national level. It is not a question of the "rights" of the developing world, but of "duties" — of the developed countries to offer assistance, and of the developing countries to ensure an environment that promotes growth with equity.

These elements — interdependence, meeting basic needs, and focussing on duties — are key elements of a harmonist philosophy. The Bank's work contributes to a translation of the paradigm into action. However, further efforts are needed to define appropriate development strategies and to advance the evolution of international financial institutions.

New Strategies for Development

In the developing countries, the idea of "closing the gap" with the developed countries still has great political appeal. The technology of transportation and communication has made it unlikely that fundamentally different lifestyles can survive in different parts of the world. However, developing countries should not try to replicate the present day lifestyles of developed countries; after all, they are unsatisfactory for many people in those countries and are not sustainable on a worldwide basis. Instead, the developing countries should aim to move in the direction the developed countries are trying to go, not toward where they are today. Developing countries should pursue a "bypass strategy of development." For example, they should avoid the developed-country model of basing economic growth on intensive energy use. And they should restrain the growth of expensive welfare systems modelled after those the developed countries are now having to curtail.

All countries need to move toward styles of life that combine material progress and the application of reason with the inner joy and inner voice that are emphasized in Asia. Most promising is a strategy that would rely heavily on both the market mechanism of Adam Smith and the value system of Mahatma Gandhi. It might be called the "Adam Gandhi philosophy."

About 200 years ago, Adam Smith demonstrated that there is an underlying harmony of interests among self-seeking individuals and that such harmony can best be promoted by the invisible hand of the market. Since then, national economies have grown interdependent, and what Adam Smith said for individuals within society can now be said for countries within the world economy. A freely operating market mechanism — with free trade in goods and factors of production — is the best way to promote the economic interests of nations, separately and jointly. As in the case of individuals, so in the case of nations, some affirmative action may be necessary to correct initial disadvantages. But in the long run, the market mechanism will contribute not only to world prosperity, but also to equitable sharing of the world's resources. The rapid improvement over the last 30 years in living standards within the newly industrializing countries, especially those which have pursued trade-oriented policies, is the strongest evidence of the validity of this thesis.

While the pursuit of self-interest is not inconsistent with the promotion of global interests, the task of market forces is made much easier if the prevailing value system restrains excesses of short-run selfish interests. The excesses of capitalism have been due, not to the mechanism of prices and markets, but to a value system that idolizes conflict and greed. The market mechanism can work even more effectively if individuals are aware of the limits of their own needs and of the satisfaction of helping others.

Gandhism can be an ally of market forces in promoting shared world prosperity. Gandhi, like other religious leaders of the world, preached love and sharing and the avoidance of greed, These virtues, combined with market forces, can help in promoting a world pattern that is both sustainable and just. Restraint on greed may help in restraining wanton misuse of natural resources, and emphasis on sharing may help in correcting the initial disadvantages of some individuals and nations.

Evolving Global Institutions

The nations of the world are now bound together economically, and the international institutions charged with global responsibility for economic development and poverty need to be strengthened. Radical proposals for massive resource transfers from the North to the South are neither reasonable nor feasible, but the existing international financial institutions require substantial evolutionary changes.

The International Monetary Fund (IMF) should evolve toward a true international central bank — with the powers of currency creation that would enable it to better meet its objectives of fostering stability in prices, trade, and exchange rates. In this system, Special Drawing Rights (SDRs), an international reserve currency already issued by the IMF, would become the sole currency for reserves and international transactions, replacing the United States dollar and other currencies that are now widely used. In other words, there should be just one currency for all international transactions.

By acting as the world's central banker, the United States borrows massively, at zero interest, from all the countries that keep dollars on hand. But as the United Kingdom learned at the end of World War II after more than half a century of serving as the world's central banker, this can distort a nation's domestic economic management and become a devastatingly heavy burden for any one nation.

The present activities of the World Bank also need to evolve. More official financing and transfers of technology are needed to help develop global infrastructure, alleviate poverty, and address the world's long-term energy problems. There are a number of potential new sources of funds that could be tapped. One is that a portion of the centrally created SDRs could be allocated specifically for development purposes, without any cost to any particular nation. Another is for the development agency to have the power to directly tax rich people around the world, those in the developing countries as well as those in the industrial countries. With these funds, the World Bank — or a new institution that would be more broadly representative and less tied to governments — could provide grants or grant-like loans (with low interest and long repayment periods) for poverty alleviation projects — water supply, vaccinations, low-cost housing, and family planning — in all countries, not only in the low-income developing countries. This institution should make these funds available not only to governments, but also to nongovernmental organizations, including charitable organizations.

The World Bank's current program of studies and investments in the energy sector should, in time, be dramatically broadened to include other resources. The world will eventually need an international institution to help develop, recycle, and conserve mineral resources, notably petroleum. Those activities should be financed by borrowings from the high-income oil exporting countries and by taxation of those who are extracting resources.

If the international transfer of resources were organized along these lines, the developed nations would not need to give aid, trade, or debt concessions to developing nations. International aid would be from the rich anywhere to the poor anywhere, which makes more precise ethical sense than providing aid on the basis of low average levels of income. In this process, non-governmental organizations could play a more important role than governments.

These ideas are visionary and idealistic and may seem remote from the hard realities of the world. However, we are at a stage of history when hard-headed marginal adjustments are not enough; we need breakthroughs in vision and idealism. I believe that progress will come, however bleak and dangerous the present outlook may be, because of the innate, though potential, goodness of mankind. If it is true that the evolutionary process includes spiritual, as well as biological development, this goodness will — inevitably — manifest itself in time. The challenge to us is to help it happen sooner rather than later. Discussions such as those that take place on Friday mornings at the Bank — among experts, politicians, and concerned citizens — can help speed up the process and avoid unproductive detours.

Sober Prospects and Christian Hope

David Beckmann

I was shaped from infancy by the Christian gospel of God's love. My parents were extraordinarily loving, and I always knew that God was the wellspring of their love. We were part of a parochial Lutheran denomination and lived in a quiet Nebraska city, but my parents were open to new ideas and the wider world. The Christian message I learned as a child, about the grace of God revealed in Jesus Christ, has remained the foundation and deepest joy of my life. This joy is still supported by a warm and solid family life, now primarily with my wife and sons.

I went to college during the years of the Vietnam War and the Black Power movement. Like many students then, I became acutely aware of injustices within the United States and in our relations with developing countries. After college I travelled in Asia and lived in Africa. I spent a year in my home state of Nebraska trying to "make the revolution"; I taught classes on current political issues and helped to get local university students and labor union leaders to meet together. Because the needed social changes went deeper than political education and organizing, I decided to enter seminary.

Upon graduation from seminary, my church asked me to be a "missionary-economist" — to help relate Christian faith to economic issues, especially Third World poverty. Graduate study of economics taught me about the complexities of trying to manipulate supply and demand to produce ethically desirable results. Work experience, starting with a stint in northwest Bangladesh, added to my respect for the complexity of social problems.

A few years after I came to the Bank, the authors of this book started the Friday morning group. The group has become a major influence in my life. Our discussions have taught me how much I have to learn from the religious experience and insights of other people. I am still convinced that Jesus is God's definitive word in the world, but I used to imagine that this somehow meant that *I* ought to have the last word in religious discussions. Gradually, I have come to appreciate how much people from other religious traditions have to teach me. In addition, the Friday group has given me a more wide-ranging understanding of global issues.

This essay argues that the survival of the world's current civilization, and perhaps of humanity itself, depends on shaping our unfolding history to a more ethical pattern. I turn to the Old Testament prophets for help in understanding the danger, to dialogue with other religions for appreciation of the universality of ethics, and to the Christian gospel for motivation and hope.

The Need for Change

The survival of human civilization is now threatened on several fronts. Yet we are failing to devote adequate effort to dealing with these threats. Most obviously, nuclear war would undermine the planet's capacity to sustain human life. The dramatic movement toward reform throughout the Communist world has given us a historic opportunity to reduce the risk of nuclear war. For 40 years, confrontation between the Soviet Union and the United States posed the main risk of nuclear war. On one side of the superpower balance, the Soviet Union was dictatorial, militaristic, and relatively isolated. On the other side, the United States in the 1980s accelerated the arms race and intensified the Cold War.

There are still many sources of conflict in the world, of course. A growing number of countries have nuclear arms, and it seems only a matter of time until terrorists get them too. The process of reform in Communist countries itself opens up new possibilities for violence among ethnic groups and over the course of reform. Yet the reform movement, however halting and turbulent it may prove to be, has dissolved the ideological underpinnings of the Cold War. The superpowers have made important progress in negotiating arms reductions. They are cooperating to control or scale down several national and regional conflicts.

We should be pursuing these possibilities much more vigorously. When Iraq invaded Kuwait in 1990, the U.S. government moved immediately and massively to put armed forces in Saudi Arabia and mobilize an international effort to restrain Iraq. This rapid response to a threat of war was necessary. But why hasn't the United States moved with the same eagerness to seize post-Cold War opportunities for peace? More vigorous efforts might have brought further progress in arms negotiations. More vigorous efforts might well have helped to build peace in El Salvador, Cambodia, the Horn of Africa, or even southern Africa. We might have helped to address long-standing problems (such as Palestinian grievances) which make any conflict in the Middle East more explosive.

Military expenditures worldwide total about one trillion dollars a year. That is much more than the *total* income of the low-income developing countries, which together represent half of the world's population. Instead we plunged into a war that wasted many lives and cost up to a billion dollars a day.

More than a billion people in the world survive on less than the equivalent of one dollar a day. People at such low levels of income usually cannot afford enough food to live fully productive, energetic lives. Infant and child mortality is high, because of poor nutrition, poor medical care, and contaminated drinking water. The persistence of poverty and hunger on such a massive scale is, after the risk of nuclear war, the second most important ethical challenge our generation faces.

Mass poverty adds to the risk of global war, because poverty invites violence, especially when the poor are getting poorer. Central America and Iran both illustrate how inequitable development, followed by recession, can set the stage for political violence with potential for superpower confrontation.

Iraq's invasion of Kuwait was spurred, in part, by regional inequalities and economic frustrations. The feasibility of economic and social progress in the developing countries has been amply demonstrated. The average income of people in the developing countries doubled in real terms between 1950 and 1980. Some newly industrialized and oil-exporting developing countries achieved a generation of economic growth unprecedented in human history. Even in the low-income developing countries, average income went up by 50 percent, the proportion of adults who could read increased from one-fifth in 1950 to two-fifths in 1980, and life expectancy jumped from 35 to 50 years. These achievements were due mainly to concentrated efforts in the developing countries, but the industrial countries helped by reducing their barriers to imports and by expanding foreign aid.

The 1980s have been a difficult decade for most developing countries. Some of the hard-earned social gains of the previous decades have been reversed. Global recession and the international debt crisis in 1982 broke the momentum of economic progress. Economic crisis had one positive effect. It discredited many authoritarian regimes and provoked a trend toward democracy among the developing countries. Much of Asia achieved rapid economic recovery and is now enjoying rapid growth again. But economic prospects remain poor throughout Latin America and sub-Saharan Africa.

A number of developing countries are now paying more to service their debts than they receive in new investment and aid. The prices of many developing-country products are at low levels, and developing countries face growing trade protectionism in the industrial countries. Under these circumstances, it is no wonder that many developing countries are in crisis. The wonder is that so few people in the industrial countries care enough about faraway poverty to insist that their governments adopt trade and financial policies that would assist hard-pressed developing countries.

Poverty has been on the rise within the United States as well. One in seven Americans lives below the poverty line. Among Blacks and Hispanics, it is one in three. The incidence of poverty is highest among children, but resources for child nutrition programs and for education have declined sharply. Homelessness is a national scandal.

The global economic difficulties of the 1970s and 1980s forced tough choices in public policy. In the United States, we chose to attack inflation, cut taxes and simultaneously build up our military — at the cost of prolonged recession and high interest rates, debts for our children, and reduced spending for the poor. We have been willing to tolerate high unemployment and growing poverty both domestically and internationally.

Environmental problems pose a third risk to human civilization. Technological power is outstripping nature's regenerative capacity. We see this repeatedly at both local and national levels — in the polluted air of our cities, for example, or in massive oil spills.

More ominous are clear signs of environmental overload at the planetary level. There is now scientific consensus that various chemicals emitted by industrial civilization are damaging the earth's atmosphere. Chlorofluorocarbons (CFCs), a family of chemicals used in industrial processes, have punched holes in the layer of ozone which protects us from the sun's harshest rays. An accumulation of various chemicals, led by carbon dioxide from the burning of fossil fuels, is trapping the sun's rays in the atmosphere. This will raise temperatures worldwide, resulting in unpredictable changes in climate and perhaps the flooding of coastal areas (as the ocean heats up slightly and expands).

Meanwhile, rapid population growth among the poor is straining nature's capacity in some developing countries. Poor people in search of land are migrating into the world's few remaining tropical forests and onto marginal lands. Their attempts to cultivate these areas are destroying the forest and creating deserts, undermining their own basis of sustenance. By one estimate, we are losing a quarter of the earth's biodiversity in the course of one human generation, and much of this is due to the loss of tropical forests.

In the developing countries, environmental protection depends heavily on slowing population growth, which in turn depends in part on improvements in social welfare. Educational opportunities for girls and reductions in infant mortality are especially important in reducing population growth. But current financial pressures restrain spending on education, health, family planning, and environmental protection.

The basic environmental question in the industrial countries is whether we are willing to consume less now to safeguard resources for the future. We cannot know what the full cost of dealing with such challenges as global warming will be. But our experiences with higher oil prices suggest that conserving resources need not spell the end of economic growth. Higher oil prices in the 1970s provoked major investments in energy conservation. These investments were expensive, but they allowed economic growth to continue according to a less energy-intensive pattern. Over the next generation we could make still more shifts away from non-renewable resources without ending the kinds of innovations and efficiencies that in the past resulted in gradual, widespread increases in economic well-being.

Some, including Ram Agarwala and Sven Burmester in this volume, argue that most people in the industrial countries would be better off with lower levels of income. I disagree. More income, wisely spent, could further improve the education we give our children, for example, or alleviate the financial constraints on providing nursing care for the elderly. But much of the economic affluence achieved since World War II has been spent in crazy and self-destructive ways. Materialistic culture encourages us to seek happiness and a sense of self-worth through acquiring and spending. Millions of people who have been tricked by these false hopes feel frustrated with their lives.

At the same time, crass materialism drains away tremendous amounts of human energy and physical resources that might be channeled into solving the problems that threaten our world. Countries and individuals fantastically rich by historical and international standards feel they cannot afford to spend much time or money on efforts to reduce poverty. While Rome burns, we fiddle with video equipment.

The problems that threaten human survival are global, but that no longer makes them remote. Through television, victims of famine in Africa and student demonstrators in China now speak directly to people in Montana and Mississippi. What happens in the United States — whether a change in interest rates or a shift in public opinion — often affects the whole world.

The world's problems are complex and controversial, but complexity should not obscure their ethical aspect. The planet's predicament is not primarily that our problems are too complicated. Rather it is that we do not have enough moral motivation to tackle world-threatening problems wholeheartedly or to seize promising opportunities. Our moral lethargy stems from problems in our inner life.

Religious Resources for Change

The Prophetic Warning

It does not take a prophet to discern that our security and prosperity depend in large part on vigorous and creative ethical action, but the Old Testament prophets confirm and clarify the challenge we face. They taught that God is the source of all blessing. Military might and economic productivity could not, they argued, assure the security and prosperity of the people of Israel. The kings should lead the nation in right worship and godly living, including social justice. The nations of Israel and Judah should try to discern and follow what the Lord was doing in their times, and then trust him for continued blessings.

As recorded in the biblical books of Deuteronomy through Kings, the kingdoms of Judah and Israel generally ignored this advice. Their history came to be characterized by a widening gap between rich and poor, and then by coups and counter-coups among competing claimants to the throne. Weakened by internal strife, they suffered piecemeal conquest by foreign powers.

These kingdoms lost the moral legitimacy they needed to elicit internal loyalty. That loss is part of what the prophets meant when they said that God was judging Israel and Judah for their sins. The prophets believed that God plays an active role in history, but also that the speaking of God's word alone has power to shake kingdoms or give hope. The prophet Amos, for example, violently condemned Israel's elite. He said they were selling "the poor for silver and the destitute for a pair of shoes," and that God would destroy Israel through the armies of an enemy nation. The priest of the royal temple told the king, "Amos is conspiring against you in Israel, and the country cannot tolerate what he is saying."

I fear that the same pattern of self-serving leadership, injustice, demoralization, and conflict is being repeated in our own time. Today's rich and powerful nations breed worldwide resentment when they neglect global problems. They also weaken their capacity to inspire self-sacrifice among their own citizens and thus become vulnerable to internal dissension. This is how ancient Israel and Judah unravelled from within. But what is at stake is no longer the destiny of just one nation, since the nations of the world are now joined together to an unprecedented degree. We risk not only the leveling of cities or the destruction of a nation, but also the annihilation of huge regions and, possibly, of virtually all living things on earth.

In the industrial democracies, many people have become skeptical of public institutions and no longer believe that their nations stand for good in the world. These countries face no greater threat to national security than disillusionment among their own citizenry. More dramatically, countries that have been under Communist rule are deeply unsettled, as citizens recoil against decades of official deceit and repression.

Both Communist and Western countries have experienced efforts to revive old-fashioned nationalism and ideology. But these are narrow, dangerous, and brittle sources of inspiration. What is needed instead is continuous effort by relatively rich and powerful countries, in both the East and West, to make the world more ethical. If the world order is flexible and serves humanity, or is at least evolving in positive directions, it will inspire the loyalty and sacrifice needed to keep it stable. Within the world's leading nations, nationalist loyalties will then be consistent with and reenforced by basic human values and a sense of responsibility to people everywhere.

The same judgment that revealed itself in the history of ancient Israel and Judah now hangs over global civilization. The Bible teaches that the Lord is patient, but unwilling forever to tolerate amorality in the making of history.

The Universality of Ethics

In modern pluralistic societies people are often reticent to speak about religion and ethics in connection with public policy. In these societies, secular traditions evolved in reaction to bitter interreligious conflicts of the past, and economic and political institutions are divorced from religious institutions and ideology. Within secular institutions, people are expected to respect religious pluralism and remain quiet about religious differences. This makes it easier for people of different convictions to live and work together.

But the habit of keeping quiet about what is most important also leads to problems. Economic and political affairs tend to proceed independently of ethical principles, and religion is relegated to oases of private meaning. Thus it is important to recognize the extent to which people from very different religious and cultural traditions share some values in common. The near universality of some values provides a basis for a civil, yet ethically charged, debate about public issues.

People everywhere agree on traditional values such as honesty and concern for others. Different cultures interpret these values differently, but virtually all peoples agree they are fundamentals of right behavior. In addition, the world's peoples now also share "modern" social ideals such as progress and rationality. These ideals were first clearly articulated at the time of the Industrial Revolution and the Enlightenment. They have spread through the world with the realization that it is possible to make life in this world better by technological improvement and the deliberate reordering of social systems. Once people realize that poverty can be overcome, for example, traditional concern for others turns into support for development and social reform. That is why Hinduism, Buddhism, Christianity, and Islam have all come to incorporate modern ideals in their contemporary ethical teaching.

The horrors of the twentieth century have made us less confident about modern social ideals. For many, words like "progress" and "rationality" connote the self-centered optimism of nineteenth century Europe and North America. But in tempered form, these ideals nevertheless infuse contemporary culture on a worldwide basis. Not even counter-culture movements in the industrial countries or virulently anti-Western movements (in Iran, for example) completely reject modernity. In fact, the world enjoys a fairly extensive moral "constitution" (a term whose Latin root means "to stand together") for secular discussion of public issues. In the World Bank, where people from many nations work side by side, it is not difficult to argue for one course of action over another by appealing to ethical values we nearly all share in common.

The main line of Christian theology confirms that the basic ethical norms spelled out in the Bible (most succinctly in the Ten Commandments) are not unique to the biblical tradition. Roman Catholicism teaches that much of ethics is "natural law," built into the character of human society. Similarly, my own Lutheran tradition teaches that God reveals part of himself — what Martin Luther called "the left hand of God" — in the laws of nature and human society. Luther would say God's "left hand" is at work when robbery leads to jail or when social injustice leads to violence. You do not need to believe in Jesus to know the difference between right and wrong or to find credible the Old Testament message of moral choice and judgment.

If Christians had a peculiar or sectarian ethic, efforts to apply it as a general norm in pluralistic, secular societies would be divisive and unfair. But since biblical values are consistent with universal human values, the Bible's prophetic tradition can speak directly and credibly to the modern world.

The Christian Gospel

Christianity's distinctive message is about the grace of God. Christians believe God came into history in the person of Jesus Christ. Jesus chose to suffer at the hands of violent people rather than forcibly resist. In the death of Jesus, God was recapturing control of his creation in a surprising way — not by a display of power, but by forgiveness and love. The resurrection of Jesus gives us hope that forgiveness and love will finally triumph.

Whether Jesus is alive at the heart of the universe is a matter of faith. But it is a matter of fact that the Christian church began when Jesus' disciples became convinced that

God had raised him from the dead. The movement they started has spread throughout the world the message that love is the ultimate, most powerful reality. Whether the love manifested in Jesus will finally prevail in the world is also a matter of faith, but it is a matter of fact that many people are touched and sometimes dramatically changed by the Christian story of God's love.

God's grace, which was especially revealed in Jesus, is what Martin Luther called God's "right hand." Grace is another way God deals with people and is quite different from what we usually observe of God in nature and history. We observe cause and effect or, more specifically in ethical matters, sin and judgment. But the gospel teaches that God has forgiven our sins, and that he will somehow free the whole world from the grim judgments of the prophets.

This prayer from the New Testament letter to the Ephesians (3:14–19) expresses a Christian's experience of the love of God:

> I kneel in prayer to the Father, from whom every family in heaven and on earth takes its name, that out of the treasures of his glory he may grant you strength and power through his Spirit in your inner being, that through faith Christ may dwell in your hearts in love. With deep roots and firm foundations, may you be strong to grasp, with all God's people, what is the breadth and length and height and depth of the love of Christ, and to know it, though it is beyond all knowledge. So may you attain to the fullness of being, the fullness of God himself.

God's love is tremendously satisfying, like intimate human love, but unconditional and with complete knowledge. The experience affects every aspect of Christians' lives, including our approach to world affairs. It provides powerful moral motivation, which is precisely what the world so urgently needs. Jesus' love inspires Christians to be uneasy with violence and inequity, even when these are socially sanctioned or seem the best that can be expected under difficult circumstances.

The Spirit's presence is evident in the passion for justice that is stirring within the churches of Latin America, most notably the Catholic church in Brazil. Scandalized by the excesses of military dictatorship in the 1970s, church leaders moved away from their historic establishment role and became critics of Brazil's severe economic inequalities. They shifted many priests and nuns from work among the privileged classes to work among the poor. Over the years, religious workers have helped to develop tens of thousands of "base communities." In these little groups, poor people gather to worship God and organize themselves to overcome poverty and injustice.

In some times and places, churches bolster forces of repression and hate. More often, churches are boring. But the Spirit sometimes breaks through in world-shaking ways — against tyranny in Poland or in the Philippines, for peace in El Salvador and Nicaragua, or against poverty in myriad church-sponsored community development projects throughout the world.

In the United States, the churches have often taken the lead in community development among low-income groups. Martin Luther King, Jr. remains a uniquely compelling example of struggle against domestic poverty and injustice. U.S. churches have also gradually become more effective in relating to poverty on a global scale. In the 1950s, they began to work systematically in the developing countries through organizations such as Catholic Relief Services and Church World Service. In the 1960s, the Vatican and World Council of Churches began to address public policy questions of importance to international development. In the 1970s, U.S. churches began to lobby Congress regarding international development. They established organizations such as Bread for the World, a Christian citizen's movement organized by both congregation and congressional district.

Such efforts may seem paltry in comparison to global problems. Yet highly motivated people are often surprisingly effective and provide spiritual leadership for the efforts of others. Those of us who believe that Jesus was

God's decisive revelation of himself expect history to be redeemed by long-suffering love rather than by displays of earthly power.

Christian experience of God's grace adds to my hope for humanity. God waited for centuries before he finally moved to destroy Israel and Judah. I trust his patience to give our world better odds than the risks we have created suggest. Day after day and decade after decade, God surprises us. The Bible promises that He has plans for humanity, within history and beyond it, which are finer than we deserve or can imagine. This promise does not mean that we can relax. On the contrary, hope that there is still time should give us both the courage to face up to the risk of self-destruction and the energy to change our ways.

The sudden emergence of democracy in many developing countries and of both political and economic reform in many Communist countries, really has seemed a gift from God. It presents us with what the Bible calls a *kairos*, a moment in which God has acted to save his people and calls on them to respond.

A Parson at the World Bank

I have been a staff member of the World Bank for 14 years. But I am also a Lutheran pastor and, in response to my call from the church, work to bring Christian faith and moral teaching to bear on global problems. When I came to the World Bank, I expected to stay a few years. But my work there has proved to be consistent with my call from the church. The Bank is a powerful, secular institution. But its objectives are ethical: economic development and poverty reduction in the developing countries. Rational and moral arguments often carry the day in its decisions.

In the early 1980s, I became concerned that the proportion of the Bank's activities focused directly on poverty reduction was declining. Economic crisis in many countries meant the Bank had to provide more help to governments in their efforts to recover financial stability and economic growth. I was writing speeches for the Bank's president at the time, and felt we needed to clarify how the Bank would maintain its special interest in poverty reduction under these difficult conditions. I wrote a paper that stimulated discussion of the issue among the Bank's top management.

I also became concerned that the Bank was not well connected with the many religious and humanitarian groups that are working to reduce poverty and hunger around the world. The Bank agreed to put me to work strengthening its relations with religious and humanitarian groups. To their great credit, my supervisors were less interested in public relations than in listening and responding substantively to issues. We brought leaders from religious and humanitarian groups to the Bank, and many of them urged more attention to activities that directly benefit poor people. UNICEF and other international institutions also sounded the alarm about what the international development crisis of the 1980s was doing to poor people. Within the Bank, several members of the Friday group were leaders of efforts to grapple with how best to help poor people in hard-pressed countries. Before too long, Bank policy shifted to reemphasize poverty alleviation.

I was then asked to help manage the Bank's relations with environmental groups. Groups such as the Environmental Defense Fund and the National Wildlife Federation criticized the Bank for not paying more attention to the environmental effects of its projects. I was allowed to work, as I had on the poverty issue, to get the Bank to respond substantively to these concerns. This interaction helped prepare for the ambitious environmental action program which the Bank launched in 1987.

At the start of 1988, the Bank began a systematic effort to involve nongovernmental organizations (NGOs) in its operations. I have led a small team which fosters and helps to guide this engagement. NGOs are now involved in about 50 of the Bank's projects each year, up from about 15 projects a year in the past. Most of the NGOs involved are grassroots groups in the developing countries — farmers' associations, women's groups, religious organizations, and indigenous social and environmental advocacy groups. The Bank works mainly with governments, but NGOs can help make official programs more responsive to low-income people. At the same time, some NGOs can expand their impact by influencing government programs and policies. The growing influence of NGOs and the spread of democracy in developing countries are related and mutually reinforcing developments, and I have recently been asked to lead a program of action and learning to strengthen the Bank's support for popular participation in development decisions.

There are several lessons from my work at the Bank that may be helpful to others. First, I have been surprised that the power of the Spirit in a secular bureaucracy is real and palpable. When the Spirit of Christ has pushed me to take a few bureaucratic risks, I have repeatedly achieved more change than I expected. Moral arguments have struck a responsive chord in all sorts of people throughout the organization. My work has not led to especially rapid promotion for me. Jesus' career does not suggest that following him will get me to the top of the bureaucratic ladder. But religiously motivated people working in other secular institutions might nevertheless take courage from my experience.

Second, the Friday group has been a continuing source of encouragement and intellectual clarity in my efforts to link faith and the Bank's work. Our group is in many ways like thousands of other voluntary fellowships around the world: Bible study groups, book-reading and discussion groups, personal support groups, and so on. But thanks to the World Bank setting, the Friday group brings together extraordinarily diverse cultural backgrounds and focuses on global issues. The group is united by a radically ecumenical, yet religious, sense of common purpose. I am convinced we have been led by the Holy Spirit, although most people in the group would not use such language.

Similar groups could form in many other situations, especially in institutions and cities with people from various national and religious backgrounds. Such groups could help mobilize the ethical energies that are often trapped in secular institutions.

A few staff members of the International Monetary Fund came to our meetings and then started their own group. The Fund group's discussions have also been wide-ranging, but they have evidenced a special interest in practical possibilities to encourage international peace. The Fund group has also discussed how the Fund's programs affect poor people. Member governments have never given the Fund a strong mandate to examine the social impact of its programs. But the Fund's management has become increasingly concerned about the impact of its programs on poverty, and our sister group is playing a modest, informal, but significant supportive role at the staff level.

A final lesson from my work at the World Bank is the importance of citizen activism on issues of global concern. Citizen activism has sharpened the Bank's focus and effectiveness on poverty and environmental problems. The world's most important issues are both moral and political, and citizen activism is often crucial in translating moral motivation into political decisions. Citizen activism is needed in every country and indeed seems to be growing in scale and sophistication in many parts of the world. Stronger organizations of poor people themselves are especially important to progress against poverty.

Citizen activism in the United States is also crucial. U.S. citizens can have a direct influence on national policy, and the U.S. government is a world leader on most global issues. Although the United States no longer dominates the world as it did in the 1950s, it still has virtual veto power on global issues. If it drags its feet in addressing the debt of developing countries, for example, other nations are unlikely to mobilize the will or resources for bold solutions at the global level.

The political forces of self-interest are stronger than the

forces of conscience. Washington, D.C., is a maze of lobbies, lawyers, and interest groups. More than 3,000 associations are headquartered in the Washington area, employing more than 80,000 workers. The bulk of these represent private interests. Organizations which represent global interests are relatively few and underfunded. Bread for the World, the churches' largest lobbying group on domestic and international poverty issues, has an underpaid staff of about 50 people.

Yet recent history has shown how public concern can build across the United States and the world, change mind sets, and then change policy: the civil rights movement in the 1950s; movements for peace, social justice, women's rights, and the environment in the 1960s; the resurgence of conservatism in the 1970s and early 1980s; and renewed concern about nuclear risk and global environmental problems in the 1980s. In every case, the grass roots led, and officialdom followed. The resurgence of democracy in many countries in recent years has dramatically demonstrated the power of ordinary people to initiate political change.

I am especially eager to see the emergence of an effective global movement to end mass hunger. Concerned people need to give more time and money to organizations that are working against hunger, especially those which address public policy. The various anti-hunger groups need to collaborate more closely, join forces with the environmental movement, and deepen their ties with grassroots organizations in the developing countries. Finally, more hunger activists need to become knowledgeable about global economic links such as debt and trade, since these links powerfully affect poor people.

On this and other pressing issues of our time, I look with great hope to the churches in the United States. Christianity has repeatedly demonstrated its capacity to spawn movements of social reform and give them staying power. The churches are already grappling with global problems—preachers are talking about them; Sunday schools are studying them; and national church offices are underwriting programs of public education and political action.

But to do our part in meeting the threats and opportunities which confront humanity, U.S. Christians will need to draw more deeply on the spiritual resources we have been given and to channel more of our spiritual energies into dealing with global ethical issues.

Can the Twilight of the Gods Be Prevented?

Beyond Faith in Science

Sven Burmester

I was born in a provincial Danish town at the beginning of World War II. The war was a devastating experience for Europe morally as well as materially. Old values that had been advanced in Denmark by the Lutheran State Church, to which more than 90 percent of the population belongs, were no longer credible. The Church and the state had worked together to indoctrinate the population in the values of duty, faith, and loyalty to King and country. But by the end of World War II, increasing cynicism about the role of ethics in world affairs made the Church less believable.

The secular trend that already characterized Europe's Social Democratic Labor parties was reinforced by the need for the war-stricken countries to work themselves out of poverty through material progress. Spiritual values did not seem relevant in this environment, but science and technology did. In my own lifetime, Denmark has gone from war-created poverty to a standard of living that sociologists say is the highest in the world.

In my childhood home, we could afford to heat only one

room in the severe winters of the 1940s; we had no hot water, and each child had only one set of clothing. Today every Danish home has central heating and children never wear the same clothes on two consecutive days. The Social Democrats for whom my middle-class family faithfully voted clearly outdistanced the Church in providing the Danes with a better, but not necessarily a happier, life. In recent years, many Danes have come to believe that material progress does not necessarily create happiness; a few have realized that spiritual progress may do so.

My father had a small print shop and was personally interested in books and languages. He was fairly fluent in both German and English and could talk with the sailors on the coal ships that came to my hometown from Newcastle. I dreamed about visiting England sometime. Little did I know that my dreams would be fulfilled beyond my wildest expectations, and that I would one day circle the globe routinely as part of my job at the World Bank.

When I graduated from high school in 1959, science and technology seemed to be the path to the future. Two years earlier the Soviets had placed the first Sputnik in orbit and ten years later the Americans would walk on the moon. I decided to become a scientist. I studied organic chemistry—a discipline which I later taught and in which I conducted research.

I spent two years at a small university in the Andes mountains of Peru. That experience taught me that science is not sufficient to change human prospects for the better. After the fall of the Inca empire, the Indians of the highlands of Bolivia and Peru were exploited by the Spanish conquerors and their descendants. Despite material and technological progress in the world around them, the Indians remained steeped in dire poverty, an easy prey to one revolutionary demagogue after another. The leader of the revolutionary movement at that time was a university colleague, Abimael Guzmán. His movement has developed into the infamous Shining Path, which is now bringing Peru to the brink of civil war. Because my scientific background made me intolerant of demagoguery, I felt — then as now— that he and his associates were wrong in their fanaticism.

I studied at Princeton University to add economics and political science to my kit of tools, and then found my way to the World Bank. I am convinced that the World Bank is succeeding in helping the poorer countries of the world realize their hopes for economic progress, and I have been personally enriched by learning the languages and cultures of the countries with which I have worked.

In my 19 years with the Bank, I have worked primarily with African and Asian countries. I have added Portuguese and Italian to the English, German, French and Spanish that I already knew, and have made some more or less successful attempts at Arabic, Chinese, and Bahasa Indonesia. Learning languages is my hobby, but I am also convinced that only by studying the history, culture, and language of the countries with which I work can I be successful in helping their development. When the Bank fails in its development efforts, it is often because the excellent economic and technical skills of staff members are not matched by an understanding of local cultures.

My most important experience in the Bank may have been my encounters with two towering figures in the development field: Robert S. McNamara, to whom I was personal assistant for three years when he was President of the World Bank, and Johannes Witteveen, the former Managing Director of the International Monetary Fund in whose Sufi group meetings I have participated for many years.

McNamara taught me that change comes about more readily when individuals set clear objectives and prepare and implement detailed plans of action with definite time schedules. Self-discipline and self-confidence are essential ingredients in the process.

Witteveen impressed upon me that spiritual progress is the purpose of life. Progress is possible only with individual effort through meditation. One must be involved in the daily affairs of human beings and must try to improve the lot of others, but in the end one must be indifferent to whether one is personally successful or not.

Africa has shown me the worst of poverty and hopelessness. I have seen the flies in the eyes of malnourished children in Ethiopia, and I have wondered whether Africa can ever progress as long as its population continues to increase rapidly. I have also worked with the nations of East Asia, where I have seen that development succeeds. I have become increasingly convinced that something more than material well-being is needed, both for my own development and growth and for humanity as a whole. Without a spiritual content to our individual and joint efforts for growth, our actions — however well-intended — may be fruitless.

The Watershed

I believe we may be at a watershed in human evolution. Many paths are possible, but two stand out. One course will lead to the extinction of humanity, the other to realization of the age-old dream of fulfilling human material needs. Science and technology have provided us with the means to eradicate poverty. We cannot give every human being all that he or she might want, but we could ensure that all human beings have what they need. Never before in human history has this been the case.

People always believe that the particular time in which they live is "the best of times, the worst of times." Given what we now know, we can smile over the fears that once gripped people during solar eclipses or the terror aroused by the newly invented crossbow. We know that life does not develop along a smooth and continuous line without violent disruption. To the contrary, the universe was born in a big bang, and suns and stars continue to explode and extinguish. Species have disappeared and continue to disappear: the fate of the dinosaurs could also be ours. On the other hand, evolution in combination with genetic engineering may create a being without normal human aggression and therefore more suitable than we are for living in a sustainable environment. Science and technology have helped humanity survive, but we know that their terrible power might indeed extinguish the human species.

Five major issues define the watershed we currently confront.

First, today there are at least six nuclear powers: the United States, the Soviet Union, China, India, France, and the United Kingdom. There are likely to be at least another six within a decade, including Iraq, Libya, Pakistan, and South Africa. Frightening as it was, the old balance of terror between the two superpowers kept the world stable. With more countries — with widely differing political interests — having nuclear weapons, there is greater risk that one or more will use that power. Perhaps even more frightening, nuclear material could fall into terrorists' hands and be used for blackmail.

Second, our current handling of the environment and its resources might lead to our ultimate destruction. In fact, if we continue on our present course, the question is not whether destruction will happen, but when. Acid rain, deforestation, ozone depletion, and global warming are clear signals that we are misusing and exhausting the resources of the planet. The discussion among economists is whether there can or cannot be substitution for the resources we are losing. One argument, often overlooked in the discussion, is that all resources are finite in the end. When will that end come? Some believe that crucial resources will run out in a generation or two, others that we might be able to continue substituting one source of energy for another until the sun burns out two billion years from now. While I might be even more concerned if I were certain that we would run out of essential resources within a generation, timing is not the issue. The important question is how we conceive of our relationship with nature. Are we here to exploit the earth and use up its capital? Or are we here to find an equilibrium with our fellow creatures, to live as stewards off the income that the earth can yield without destroying its capital?

Third, we are dallying with the time bomb of high population growth in the less developed countries. When population growth exceeds economic growth, people become poorer. The standard of living in most of Africa and many South Asian countries is totally unacceptable by any measure; no substantial material progress has been made. In almost all sub-Saharan African countries, per capita income today is lower than when they achieved political independence, some thirty or more years ago. In these circumstances, the risk of social and political upheaval is great.

Fourth, the international economic and financial system is in turmoil. The debt problems of both poor and rich countries — Brazil and the United States are good examples — loom large and are far from resolved. But important as this is, it is less threatening than the nuclear and environmental dangers described above. First, prudent policies can still save the system, and most likely will. Second, with an average global per capita income of $4,000 per year, one could argue that man has solved the basic economic problem and that the remaining challenge is one of adequate distribution. The prospect of some of us having to face some economic decline in our standard of living is not fateful for humanity — nuclear weapons and ecological disaster are.

Even so, we should not underestimate the truly global character of the international financial system and the importance of the link between financial and economic variables. No government can run its economy without regard for others. Reluctance of Japanese and German investors to finance the U.S. balance of payments deficit might create chaos in the U.S. economy with ripple effects throughout the world. Clearly, a shaky financial system will have real effects, and these are particularly dangerous when they spill over into unemployment and inflation.

Fifth, our national and international institutions may

no longer be able to keep up with the pace of change. In the United States, the President and Congress have been unable, despite many attempts, to reduce spending or raise taxes enough to resolve the U.S. budget problem. In a number of European countries, political parties have multiplied so that majority governments can no longer be formed. Denmark, Italy, and the Netherlands are examples. We are proud of the checks and balances in democratic systems, but a stalemate is often the result.

At the same time, the media have emerged as possibly the most powerful institution of all, but they are not subject to checks and balances. The concentration of the media on the dramatic and the immediate might prevent a better popular understanding of the real dangers facing humanity. Instead of contributing to sustained attention to complex issues, media simplify and thereby trivialize them. Television commentators call for immediate arms reduction, even though it will take years to accomplish this goal. And should we get a few cool summers, the media will lose interest in global warming, which will continue unabated as political pressure for action ceases.

Where do these issues leave us now?

Material wealth has reached heights which were undreamed of a generation ago in Europe and the United States, but happiness has not followed. There is not necessarily a close relationship between material progress and happiness, although there is probably a certain minimal threshold below which human happiness is largely precluded. That threshold corresponds approximately to the level where life expectancy is approaching 60 years (as in China today), where infant mortality is about 30 per 1000 live births, and where illiteracy is being rapidly eliminated. In dollar terms, these events tend to happen when per capita income reaches about $1000. Above that threshold, however, there seems to be little relationship between income and happiness.

A 1984 international Gallup poll indicated that people in rich countries tended to be happier than people in poorer countries. It also showed that most people considered as ideal an income about twice their present income, whatever that was. Over the last generation, the people of Europe more than doubled their incomes and their expectations were more than met. But human memory is short, and people are now preoccupied with frustration about the relatively slow economic growth of recent years.

The Scandinavian experience is interesting. Scandinavia's material development took off in the latter part of the nineteenth century. An important contributing factor was the religious awakening that took place at that time. Common people learned to read the Bible, and increased literacy led to higher productivity. With the rise of the workers' movement, however, aesthetic, cultural, and religious goals fell into the background, and material goals took precedence. Since the Depression, the movement has concentrated on shorter working hours, better working conditions, and higher pay — material aspirations that were more than met by 1970. A sense of emptiness has followed; people, particularly young people, now find it difficult to see meaning in their lives.

Western culture is perhaps overly impressed with the results of modern technology and too inclined to exalt science and technology as the only truth. Such a purely materialistic faith endangers our survival. We must be acutely conscious of how much we still do not know about who were are and where we are going. We must be careful not to freeze ourselves into one scientific paradigm, thereby excluding the possibility of radically different ones. No true scientist would ever do this. We must proceed with scientific endeavors, but we must do so, as most scientists themselves do, with humble minds.

Preventing Disaster, Protecting the Future

In view of the problems we face, what can we do? Many people would say that careful economic and political decisions, together with further scientific progress, will allow mankind to thrive and prosper. But it seems prudent to introduce changes in the behavior of governments, institutions, and individuals that will not hinder our further progress and that may help us to avoid the twilight of the gods to which nuclear war or environmental destruction will inevitably lead.

What standards should guide the changes to be made? Fundamentally, we must conserve and enhance values that are increasingly and universally agreed upon: First, the basic needs for material survival must be ensured. Second, society must function in such a way that people maintain their self-esteem and feeling of value. It is on this score that modern Western society fails, and in particular my own Scandinavia: too many people feel that they are useless and unimportant in the progress of society. Third, individual freedom — with responsibility — must be protected and extended.

What kinds of actions are necessary to conserve and enhance these basic values?

The Role of Governments, Rich and Poor

The *developed countries*' first task is to ensure that humanity does not destroy itself in a nuclear holocaust. Ultimately, this means that nuclear weapons must be abolished. A long and tortuous path of strategic arms limitation talks lies ahead. With the events of 1989, it is gratifying to note that the two superpowers now have taken the first important steps on that path. The objective must be clear: as long as we have nuclear weapons on the globe, our survival is threatened by superpower conflict or by terrorists' use of these weapons. Including conventional weapons, we spend 20 times more on trying to destroy ourselves than on trying to foster economic and social progress in the developing countries. Surely, a few more dollars for development would do more to enhance world security than if they were spent on arms.

The second task of the rich countries is to increase their

efficiency in using scarce resources. The ultimate constraint on resource use is the carrying capacity of the globe: per capita resource use should not exceed the level the globe can sustain for all the world's people. Today's per capita resource use in industrial countries is not sustainable for all inhabitants of the earth. It is obviously difficult to be precise about the carrying capacity of the planet, but various estimates — most recently by the International Commission on Development and Environment — show that the planet is capable of carrying only about 500 million people indefinitely at the level of income and technology in the United States today. If resources were used more prudently as in Europe and Japan, the planet might carry about one billion people indefinitely. Demographers estimate that, if present trends continue, the world's population (now five billion) will stabilize sometime in the twenty-first century at nine to twelve billion human beings.

The rich countries must take three steps in relation to efficient resource use. First, they must vigorously strive to use resources better and to avoid irreversible pollution of the atmosphere, water, and arable soil. Second, they must take immediate and decisive steps to assist developing countries to slow their rapid population growth rates. And third, they must assist the poor countries with economic development.

While the main responsibility for development rests with the developing countries themselves, they cannot do it alone. The middle-income developing countries (those with annual per capita incomes of more than $500) are likely to reach acceptable standards of living if they continue to have access to commercial investment and export opportunities in the markets of rich countries. But the low-income developing countries (those with annual per capita incomes below $500; that is, most sub-Saharan African countries and the poorest countries of Asia) will require continued financial assistance at concessionary terms for many years to come.

There are strong moral grounds for increasing this

assistance by cutting per capita consumption among the rich and transferring the savings to the poor. Such cuts in consumption could either be voluntary or take the form of a global tax. Many say that a global tax is not possible, yet income taxes were believed impossible in the nineteenth century and today are commonplace all over the world. In a sense, today's development assistance is a global tax, although a very small one that in the rich countries averages only 0.36 percent of national income. This is in contrast to the 2.5 percent of national income the United States contributed to finance the Marshall Plan in 1947. Is it really so far fetched to think that the level attained by the United States in 1947 could be attained today, particularly in view of the decreased international tension caused by the events in Eastern Europe? West Germany will far exceed these levels in its aid to East Germany. So why could a financial effort not be made globally?

Whatever the rich countries do, the fact remains that interdependence among countries of the world is increasing. Modern communications and trade bind the world together more closely than ever before. For example, if a bad harvest in the Soviet Union leads the United States to sell more grain to the Soviets, the price of food worldwide increases, and a landless laborer in Bangladesh is likely to become even hungrier than he was before.

So far as the *developing countries* are concerned, their overriding preoccupation should be to fulfill the basic material needs of their people. Self-esteem and freedom are unlikely to be achieved as long as basic material needs are not met. Several developing countries in Latin America and East Asia are well on their way to reaching the goal of meeting basic needs, but the majority of nations in Sub-Saharan Africa and South Asia are still far from doing so.

This goal will be reached more easily if population growth is slow; hence, reducing that growth is of crucial importance to developing countries. While most couples in rich countries consider it in their own interest to have small families, many couples in developing countries feel that a large number of children provide both farm labor today and security in old age. Government policies to slow population growth must address this issue.

While economic development should take place as fast as possible in the developing countries, environmental protection should be an important concern as well. But the major polluters of the world today are the rich countries, and the major responsibility for preventing environmental degradation and the eradication of the species remains with them.

The Role of the World Bank

The World Bank is only one of many institutions that address the problems considered here. The Bank's Articles of Agreement limit it to dealing with world economic issues. It cannot, therefore, participate in the political debate on nuclear weapons or the weakness of democratic institutions. But it can — and does — play a vigorous role in reducing population growth in developing countries and in protecting the environment from excessive exploitation. While one might also wish that the Bank would take an active stand on human rights issues, strict adherence to economic principles has served the Bank and the world community well. It is therefore lamentable that the rich member countries forced the Bank to violate its own principles by denying loans to China.

The Bank view is that high population growth rates, especially in Africa, are a major obstacle to meeting the basic needs of people in the poorest countries. It is committed to ensuring the long-term per capita income growth that will lift these countries out of poverty. At the same time, the Bank has a large Catholic and Muslim constituency and must be both patient and cautious in the population field.

The Chinese population policy — with its simultaneous emphasis on contraception, including forced abortion, and education of girls and women — has been the most successful in the world. But it has been both painful and controversial. Short-term pain, however, is often necessary for long-term gain, and the Bank, through its structural adjustment lending as well as its direct lending for population, should put pressure on governments to adopt objectives for population growth rates similar to those of the Chinese. The means could be less drastic than in China, and rely more heavily on education of girls and women. But without dramatic declines in present growth rates, the poorest countries are doomed to continued misery.

The Bank entered the environmental debate fairly late and has to take its share of the blame for earlier mistakes. But it is now geared up for greater involvement in environmental issues: it has technical expertise on environmental issues in each of its regional offices and created an environment department to provide intellectual support at the policy level. The Bank is also increasingly supportive of non-governmental organizations active on environmental issues.

The Bank's influence on solving environmental problems will remain limited, however, because the rich countries are the worst polluters and the Bank has no influence on their policies. While deforestation and desertification in developing countries may be alleviated through Bank assistance, such destructive phenomena as acid rain, the greenhouse effect of fossil fuel consumption, and the destruction of the ozone layer will continue unless the rich nations take action.

Lower population growth rates and an improved environment may occur as a result of policy dialogue and technical and financial assistance, if the Bank and borrowing countries can agree on appropriate policies. But these goals will not be achieved if the poor cannot understand the message because of widespread illiteracy. Education is, therefore, a necessary condition for change.

Eight of my nineteen years in the World Bank have been spent working on education projects in Africa and East Asia. I am left with a feeling of "too little, too late" in Africa, where the absolute number of illiterates has increased despite soaring increases in enrollment ratios in primary schools. Financially, the African governments cannot keep up with the ever increasing number of children. And when the children are not educated, population growth rates for the next generation will remain high. It is in the interest of everyone to provide African education systems with the necessary finance to break this vicious cycle and ensure education for all children.

In East Asia the cycle has been broken. Population growth rates are coming down in part because of better education of girls. For example, in Indonesia, where enrollment of girls in primary education has increased from 65 percent in 1965 to virtually universal enrollment in the late 1980s, population growth declined from about three percent to 1.7 percent over the same period. Better education is also increasing environmental awareness, particularly in China.

The Power of Individual Action

Ultimately, we will either perish or establish a world civilization. This is a strong statement. But separate states, separate religions, separate ideologies are simply not compatible with sustainable development.

Governments cannot create a world civilization. Governments in the rich countries seem unable to solve the economic problems that beset them; they are increasingly rigid. As long as interest groups resist making any sacrifices to solve the problems that affect everyone, no economic policy can work. What is needed are major changes in the lifestyles, habits and attitudes of large numbers of courageous, warm-hearted, but hard-nosed individuals. The sum of individual choices and actions can be a powerful force for change.

The current emphasis on material progress is not likely to create the kind of individuals we need. Persistence in thinking that individual material progress is the road to happiness will lead to failure — because Western governments are no longer able to assure such progress, and because happiness does not necessarily come from material well-being. A change in lifestyle is not only necessary; it is also beneficial to the individual. Can that change occur? And where will it come from? Perhaps from religious faith and from faith in one's own ability to cope with problems as they arise.

In recent years a large number of Americans have stopped smoking, changed to more healthful diets, or started exercising on a regular basis. These small examples are evidence that people are both able and willing to change lifestyle when they are convinced that it is for their own good.

A more radical change in lifestyle would be a revival of the ancient practice of fasting. Millions of people in the rich countries want to lose weight. Instead of wasting money on fad diets, why should they not do as our forefathers did and stop eating when they have had enough?

Individual actions that put consumption to a level that is sustainable on a global basis are good and healthy, but these benefits should not be the main reason for undertaking them. There is a certain danger of narcissism in becoming preoccupied with oneself and one's efforts at self-improvement. The main reason is to bring about material savings that can be used for action that benefits the international society. Individual energies must be used for collective action — in the end, political action.

Neighbors who have fasted can donate the money they would otherwise have used on food to a private agency with programs of assistance in developing countries. As their understanding grows, they can put pressure on local politicians to increase economic aid to developing countries. People may express their concern about the environment by cleaning up their own neighborhood. As they realize how much trash individual households produce, they may also realize that their country is polluting the globe. That realization can lead to pressure at the political level.

People in the rich countries will enjoy their own comfortable standards of living more if they become aware of the global situation. Fasting can enhance feasting. We in the rich countries are privileged beyond belief, and the ultimate sin would be to be unconscious of our privileges and unable to enjoy them. People who seek meaning in their lives can find some meaning by concentrating on the enormous problems of people in the poor countries. The feeling in the past that one's neighbor's children also had a right to food, education, and a better standard of living contributed to material progress in many nations. It is now time to extend this solidarity to the entire globe.

Many futurists in the West believe that further progress in science and technology, particularly with respect to microprocessing and communication, will eventually solve our economic problems. They think robots will take care of all mechanical work. I do not think this is likely. My hope is that information technologies will help us acquire a more sophisticated understanding of problems. Because the human mind focuses on only one variable at a time, we tend to attribute all our problems to a single cause — inflation, tax burdens or Communism, for example. When computers become commonplace, their ability to analyze the simultaneous influence of many variables may help us develop less simplistic points of view. There is a split in modern society between the elites who understand and encourage progress and the masses who feel increasingly frustrated, confused, and left behind. If made widely available, technologies could reduce this gap, and make modern society more durable.

Individuals in developing countries also have responsibilities and possibilities for influencing the fate of humanity. Educated leaders must determine what they want the future to be. Proposals for a "new economic order" that included plans for commodity price stabilization and an international central bank represented one such effort. These proposals were not well worked out, however, and they dealt only with economic problems.

Economics should not be the sole preoccupation of leaders in the developing countries: economic dreams could easily turn into nightmares. It is unlikely that the developing countries will be able to catch up with the rich countries economically, nor is this even desirable. It is desirable and necessary, however, that all people are ensured their basic material needs. Once those needs are met, spiritual needs and the continued survival of humanity must be foremost in the minds of developing — as well as developed — country leaders.

The developing countries can contribute diversity to the future. A precondition for evolution is the existence of diverse cultures and languages. The Anglo-Saxon industrial culture that now dominates the world is not likely to be the best survival pattern for mankind as a whole. While industrialization has the capacity of giving a decent material existence to all the inhabitants of the globe for the first time in history, it is doubtful that it can give much more than that. Its success is based on the Newtonian machine-like image of the universe. This concept of the universe, although useful for its exploitation, is likely to be detrimental to its survival. Modern physics, modern biology, and modern philosophy all lean toward the ancient beliefs of the East regarding harmony as the guiding principle in the universe. If we do not learn to live harmoniously with each other, we shall perish.

Is humanity today in the most dangerous situation it has ever confronted? Jeremiah started crying wolf 2500 years ago, and the world still stands. But today's dangers may well be greater than any humanity has faced before. Individuals are likely to change their behavior and the behavior of their societies not because the world may be endangered, but because they will, in fact, be happier with a lifestyle that is not solely concentrated on material needs.

The economists who believe that present problems — environment, exhaustion of resources, and gaps between rich and poor within and among nations — can be solved by tinkering with the market here and there to get it to function better may be right. But the resulting world will not be a very pleasant one. It will be fairly rich, but it will be dirtier, more crowded, and less diversified than at present.

Economists tend to assume that people will only change if they see material improvement for themselves in such a change. History belies this assumption. The reformers who first talked about abolishing slavery and colonialism were looked upon as utopians, but their visions nevertheless came true.

Maybe some creatures from outside our earth would look upon us as a cancer that endangers the planet. In a material sense, our growth in numbers and our devouring of all available resources of the globe certainly make us look cancerous. But we are, after all, more than that. We are also spiritual beings. We have created the music of Bach, we have established the theories of Einstein, and we have had a Buddha, a Mohammed and a Jesus to tell us what our lives are about.

Even observers from outside would consider it a pity to see us disappear. They might fear our violence and our blindness, but if we can release the spiritual forces within us, I believe they would welcome us as worthy stewards of the future.

The Justly Balanced Society: One Muslim's View

Ismail Serageldin

I grew up in a civilized and secure environment where material well-being was taken for granted by the children, the social graces were held in high esteem by the parents, and culture was appreciated by all. Above all, the pursuit of knowledge, in the broadest sense, was idolized. My two sisters and I read English, French, and Arabic, on almost every subject. Conversation was substantive and sharp, almost with a debater's edge, tempered only by the civility enforced by our elders.

A pervasive internationalism complemented the deep roots my family had in Egypt. The French enlightenment, British constitutionalism, the classics and Sartre all had their place next to Islamic thought, Arab history, literature, and Muslim art. Religious ethics and tolerance were almost indistinguishable in my developing perceptions. From French period furniture to Dutch paintings to western modernist architecture, our home opened up vistas of a sense of place that was different from, and somehow complementary to, the Egypt that surrounded us. The trees and billowing clouds of European landscapes as well as artwork from the far east, Turkey, and Iran comprised a universe of far-flung horizons that nurtured a growing appetite for exploration and an eclectic taste for the beautiful.

I chose to study architecture at an early age, following in my father's and sister's footsteps. From architecture, I turned to the problems of cities, then regions, and finally entire nations, always in pursuit of the elusive causes of prevailing conditions and the means to improve them. From architecture to city and regional planning to development economics to human resource development to practicing international development assistance at the World Bank — it was a natural, logical progression. I moved from Engineering School at Cairo University to graduate studies at Harvard to professional practice. From my early interest in architecture, I retain a strong fascination with aesthetics and cultural expression that has kept me involved with architecture as critic and writer, if not practitioner, throughout the last twenty years. But gradually, my commitment to international development issues became the dominant force in my life, both professionally and as a means of living the Muslim faith as I understand it.

In tackling international development issues, my early experience is reflected in internationalist values and a pragmatic, non-doctrinaire view of the world and its economic problems. While I remain an Egyptian Muslim of the Sunni persuasion, I have been deeply influenced by western ideas and practices. This internationalism enhanced my appreciation of my Arab and Egyptian cultural heritage as part of the global culture. My exposure to socialist thought generally and Marxism specifically came during my graduate studies. While the equity and justice central to socialist thought were attractive, I found the formal materialism of Marxism repugnant to my deep commitment to spiritual values, and the repressive practices of some so-called socialist regimes gave me grounds to doubt the ethical foundations of the underlying doctrine. Therefore, on balance, western democratic ideals of personal liberty and tolerance clearly remain the dominant external influence on my thinking.

On economic doctrine, however, I harbor a dual skepticism — about the power of the market's invisible hand and the all-too-visible and heavy hand of central planning. Neither unfettered capitalism nor central planning constitute the single magic formula to solve the problems of a rapidly changing world. What worked in the United States or the People's Republic of China is not necessarily the most suitable formula for others, whose development problems and range of options are fundamentally different.

These, in a nutshell, are the views that I carried to my vocation in economic development, and that I brought to the discussions of the Friday morning group at the World Bank.

Global Madness

Any rational human being surveying the state of world affairs today must be appalled by the gross inequities in the distribution of wealth and income among nations, groups, and individuals. The most basic and fundamental of human rights are not recognized, much less respected. Mutual suspicion and outright hatred are the predominant orders of the day. The greed and aggressiveness of individuals and groups is matched by the callousness, self-interest and competitiveness among nations. The environment, our heritage, and our resources are being depleted and destroyed in a frantic pursuit of material gains, however fleeting they may be. Civilized discourse and peaceful arbitration within a framework of law are rarely found. Armed conflict appears to be the preferred means of securing the objectives of nations—foolhardy at a time when the nuclear arsenals of the world are sufficient to destroy us all many times over. If developed-country military budgets were reduced by only five percent and these amounts channeled to the developing countries, the flow of aid from the rich to the poor would double. What madness grips the human race! Two world wars and countless smaller conflicts should have been sufficient to bring forth a world community of nations. But we remain prisoners of our own folly.

As a Muslim surveying this chaotic scene, I am struck by the losses humanity has incurred, especially the loss of the universal bond that should exist among all human beings:

> O mankind! We created you of a male and a female and made you into nations and tribes that ye may know each other not that ye may despise each other. Verily the most honored of you in the sight of God is he who is the most righteous of you.
>
> (*Quran*, 49:13)

This call for universal brotherhood and righteousness is addressed to all of mankind, not just Muslims.

Yet the curse of twentieth century mankind is a new "religion" that divides rather than unites — rabid, narrow-minded nationalism. All the spiritual religions of the world have as their ultimate foundation a broad ethical framework that calls for the salvation of all mankind and emphasizes universality and tolerance. That foundation has survived many misguided attempts through the ages to persecute, colonize, and oppress others in the name of religion. Such attempts were really political movements seeking to legitimize particular doctrines by invoking the name of God.

Chauvinistic nationalism replaces the narrow loyalty of the tribe with the broader and antagonistic us/them idea of the modern state, whose boundaries are geographically defined by the accidents of history and human caprice. This nationalism is not a form of cultural expression that is so necessary in defining one's identity. It is, instead, the "statist," ethnocentric doctrine that places greater store in the "national interest" than in the interest of humanity. In the name of national interest ever deadlier armaments are obtained, neighbors threatened, and wars justified.

The absolute lack of an ethical dimension in the ideology of nationalism allows it to justify the most hideous crimes against others outside the nation, and in many cases even against citizens of the nation state itself whose actions are deemed a threat to national security. It is an ideology of selfishness, one that produced that abhorrent slogan "my country, right or wrong." Nationalism is a destructive force in world affairs today; unfortunately, it is likely to remain the dominant force in international affairs for the foreseeable future.

The loss of universal ethical values is a challenge that we are called upon to meet to the best of our abilities. Some would impose values by the force of arms. But force and coercion are fundamentally at odds with the Muslim ethical framework.

> Let there be no compulsion in religion: Truth stands out clear from error.
>
> (*Quran*, 2:256)

How, then, are we to respond to this challenge? Muslims, like all who accept universal ethical values, are called upon to play an important role among the "nations and tribes" of this world:

> Thus have we made of you a nation justly balanced that you might be witnesses over the nations and the Apostle a witness over yourselves.
>
> (*Quran*, 2:143)

The message of Islam is to help humanity by "being witnesses," not by imperial order. "Being witnesses" means to bring to bear the force of good example. Islam tells us there is to be no persecution, no intolerance, no forceful conversions to a single way. The only road open to us all is the road of reason, tolerance, and the moral force of example. The justly balanced society called for in the *Quran* is to be created by each dealing with his own weaknesses:

> O ye who believe. Guard your own souls: if ye follow right guidance, no hurt can come to you from those who stray.
> (*Quran*, 5:108)

As a Muslim from a developing country, I must try to reinstate spiritual values as guides to dealing with development problems. It is both striking and sad that "development" is perceived by most of the ruling elites of the developing countries as the process of attaining the wealth and living standards of western mass-consumption society. It is highly probable that for the vast majority of developing countries this objective is unattainable; only preposterous assumptions about future scenarios suggest it is possible. The absurdity of that objective was forcefully stated by Robert McNamara in 1977 when he rejected "closing the gap" as a measure of the success of development efforts:

> 'Closing the gap' was never a realistic objective in the first place. Given the immense differences in the capital and technological base of the industrialized nations as compared with that of the developing countries, it was simply not a feasible goal. Nor is it one today . . . Even if the developing countries manage to double their per capita growth rate, while the industrial world maintains its historical growth, it will take nearly a century to close the absolute income gap between them. Among the fastest growing developing countries, only seven would be able to close the gap within 100 years, and only another nine within 1,000 years.[1]

It is doubtful that closing the gap would be worthwhile even if it could be done. Serious analysis has raised doubts about whether the consumption practices of the industrial world could be sustained if they were practiced by all mankind. But even without these pragmatic concerns, it must surely be recognized that all that glitters is not gold, and development must mean more than the sheer accumulation of worldly goods.

The quest for a broader meaning to development should generate questions in the minds of decision-makers and the public at large, questions such as, development for what? development for whom? and are we paying too high a price for what we call development? These are not technical questions. Only a set of values, whether explicitly or implicitly defined, can provide the answers. There are no value-neutral answers to such questions. Without such questions development becomes merely a means of increasing materialism, which societies are increasingly aware they cannot afford and which the more thoughtful seek to reject.

Squirm as they will, technocrats cannot avoid confronting their values in the choices they make. Economics has never been, and cannot be, value-free or value-neutral. There are those who argue that economic analysis should speak for itself in the objective language of hard numbers. But the pursuit of hard numbers is only a mirage. Even in such "hard" sciences as biology and anatomy, scientists are not immune from their value systems, and *a priori* beliefs intrude into their work and influence their analyses.[2]

It behooves us to be candid, explicit, and up front about the values that undergird the prescriptions that we advocate.

Stewardship of the Earth

Any proposal for action must be rooted in one's system of values. I believe the starting point for action is defining the purpose of being on earth. After much reflection on the Muslim tradition, I believe that humanity has a role as "steward of the earth." The fulfillment of the role involves a test, and this test requires confronting hardship with patience and action.

The concept of "stewardship of the earth" deserves elaboration. It plays a central role in my vision of spiritual and material development. It is curiously underrepresented in the scholastic tradition of Islamic theology, although references to it are plentiful in the *Quran*.

The Arabic word, *Khalifa* (*Istakhlafa*), that I translate as "stewardship" appears in several scripture passages and has been variously translated by eminent scholars as vice-regent of god on earth, agent, inheritor, successor. To me, the concept of stewardship best captures the multi-faceted nature of the human assignment.

Stewardship is central to the very role of humanity in the cosmos. It is God's design that man should go to earth as his vice-regent:

> "Behold," the Lord said to the angels,
> "I will create
> A vice-regent on earth."
>
> (*Quran*, 2:30)

Vice-regency carries special responsibilities and gives rise to the stewardship concept:

> Then we made you heirs
> In the land after them,
> To see how you would behave.
>
> (*Quran*, 10:14)

The behavior expected of the stewards of the earth is spelled out in another passage, where God addresses David:

> "O, David. We did indeed
> Make thee a vice-regent
> On earth: so judge thou
> Between men in truth and justice . . ."
>
> (*Quran*, 35:39)

The universality of this injunction is clear in the Arabic because the word that appears here as "vice-regent" is the same as the word used for "inheritors" or "successors" in other passages addressed to all who believe in God:

> He is it that has made
> You inheritors of the earth:
> If then, any do reject
> God, their rejection works
> Against themselves.
>
> (*Quran, 35:39*)

God's grace is conditioned on the proper execution of stewardship. The assignment of stewardship is transferable from generation to generation and from group to group:

> Thy Lord is Self-sufficient
> Full of Mercy; if it were
> His will, He could destroy
> You, and in your place
> Appoint whom He will
> As your successors, even as
> He raised you up
> From the posterity
> Of other people.
>
> (*Quran,* 6:133)

Discharging the responsibility of stewardship involves the entire behavior of the believer, and hence can serve as the core that defines the right behavior for a true Muslim at all times.

The concept of stewardship of the earth has three dimensions: exercising responsibility, being tested, and enduring hardship with patience. Responsibility to God involves *responsibility* for the well being of the planet, other creatures, other human beings, and future generations as well.

In addition, stewardship involves being tested:

It is He who hath made
You His agents, inheritors
Of the earth: He hath raised
You in ranks, some above
Others: that he may try you . . .

(*Quran*, 6:165)

It may be that your Lord
Will make you inheritors
In the earth; that so
He may try you
By your deeds.

(*Quran*, 7:129)

The test recognizes that actual deeds are far more important than just words of prayer:

God has promised, to those
Among you who believe
And work righteous deeds, that He
Will, of a surety grant them
In the land, inheritance
Of power, as He granted it
To those before them.

(*Quran*, 24:55)

Because believers are accountable for their actions, behavior must be governed by conscience, not just strict adherence to laws. Believers should recognize whether their actions are fair or unfair, just or unjust, even if the actions in question are legal.

Finally, the concept of stewardship means that humanity must also bear hardships with patience and endurance, but not with fatalism or passivity.

Verily, We have created
Man in toil and struggle.

(*Quran*, 90:4)

Hardship is a call for action with no immediate rewards. It calls for perseverance and a long run perspective.

A Justly Balanced Society

The exercise of stewardship has two components. The first might be called "development of the earth." This involves taming nature to serve humanity's purpose, cultivating its resources, and increasing its bounty. But this must be done as steward, not as rapacious exploiter. Actions are balanced, with limits imposed on greed and personal ambition so that the underlying, sustaining system is nurtured. The second component of stewardship is the organization of those who work this earth and enjoy its fruits and bounty in a fair and mutually supportive manner, that is, in a "justly balanced" society.

A justly balanced society based on the principles of Islam has several broad features. First, it nourishes *freedom.* Islam is an ideology of liberation. It sets the believer free from all worldly fears and shackles. Believers communicate directly with God, without the intermediation of clergy. Islamic believers feel they are masters of their actions and will be held accountable to God alone. They give total obedience to God. Hence, obedience to worldly institutions and beings must be subject to the dictates of conscience: thus are believers set free. But their freedom is circumscribed by the bounds of law:

> O ye who believe. The law
> of equality is prescribed to you . . .
> . . . In the Law of Equality there
> is Life, to you
> ye men of understanding;
> That you may restrain yourselves.
>
> (*Quran*, 2:178)

Any society that tries to live with Islamic principles must protect the freedom and dignity of its members through a legal framework that does not allow the humiliation of anyone. This freedom applies to families as well as societies, and should be interpreted in its broadest sense.

Second, a justly balanced society promotes *the search for knowledge and truth.* The pursuit of knowledge is the single most striking feature of Islam. (The word for knowledge, *Ilm,* and its derivatives occur 880 times in the *Quran.*) But knowledge is not neutral. It is the basis for better appreciating truth (the Arabic word is *Haq*), which is revealed, but which can be perceived in the world. Indeed, believers are enjoined to look around them and to learn the truth.

The Prophet Mohammed exhorted his followers to seek knowledge as far away as China, then considered to be the end of the earth. He held scientists in high esteem, saying that the ink of scientists is equal to the blood of martyrs. The very first word of Quranic revelation is an order to read, to learn, and to seek knowledge.

Third, a justly balanced society is characterized by *action and industry,* which are the way of salvation. The faithful are enjoined to act:

> . . . and do good deeds, and your actions will be seen by God, His prophet, and the believers.
>
> (*Quran,* 9:105)

These actions should be for the common good. But even those actions which are private — whether it is a craft or intellectual endeavor — should be undertaken with discipline and precision and to produce quality work.

The Muslim faithful are responsible for other human beings, and are exhorted to redress injustice to the full extent of their abilities. As is stated in the *Hadith,* which contains the words of the Prophet and is the second most powerful source of Islamic tradition after the *Quran:*

> If one of you sees something that is wrong, then let him set it right; first with his hand, and if he cannot then with

his tongue, and if he cannot then with his heart, and that is the weakest of all possible forms of faith.

These exhortations place a heavy emphasis on being active in this world and acting well at all levels. Contemplative meditation is not an end in itself, but a means of self-renewal in order to be able to undertake more and better things in the future.

Fourth, in the justly balanced society, the concept of *justice* is absolute. For Muslims, all actions are part of the great test, in which success is defined by acting in a just manner. Islamic legislation seeks to set the limits for what is permissible between individuals, by defining a theory of rehabilitation and punishment and the exact punishment to be meted out. It is the responsibility of jurists to update and enforce the law in ways that are as perfectly just as possible. Legislative compromises that reflect the balance of power of groups or individuals are unacceptable if they infringe upon the rights of the weak. Scholars recognize that some things go beyond the means of the Muslim community and are in the hands of the Creator. But an essential feature of Muslim society is that it seeks to establish justice here on earth: justice does not wait for the Kingdom of Heaven.

Fifth, in the justly balanced society, changes are governed by *the public interest.* Under Islam, the public interest is justification for changing past forms and coping with an ever changing present and future. The pursuit of the public interest both helps and checks new legislative innovations. For example, inter-regional trade agreements or new financial instruments can be promoted on the grounds of the public interest. On the other hand, legislative innovations that benefit the few at the expense of the public at large, such as land-grant concessions that irretrievably damage the environment by deforestation or strip-mining, can be rejected on the same grounds.

The liberal interpretation of this concept is "All that is not expressly forbidden is allowed." In every Muslim society, numerous mechanisms and processes have been worked out in great detail to ensure that new initiatives are still consonant with the ethical principles of the *Quran*, and that evolution does not, over time, lead to the abandonment of the basic ethical principles set out in the original seventh century society in Medina.

Finally, because justice must be tempered by mercy, a justly balanced society exhibits *compassion for the poor and weak*. The faithful are enjoined to show mercy toward those who are less fortunate, to show compassion to the needy, to be magnanimous in victory, and to be forgiving when in power. The Muslim system was the first to introduce a form of social security and welfare assistance whereby the poor and the weak had a *right* to part of the public treasury and did not have to rely on charity. *Zakat* is a taxation of the rich, with the poor having an absolute right to the proceeds. Prescribed in the *Quran*, it was established from the earliest days of the Prophet in Medina.

While these principles are essential to Islam, many have proved hard to follow and Muslim societies have had governments as venal and tyrannical as others. But the message of these principles remains to inspire generation after generation of reformers who seek to interpret in contemporary terms this profound commitment to the justly balanced society.

A development pattern consonant with the principles of Islam will require a completely new approach that differs fundamentally from the traditional western neo-classical economic approach in two important respects. First, it requires a holistic view of development — social, political, cultural, physical, and economic — and second, it is focused on human beings, not on economics alone.

This focus on people represents a major departure from the mainstream of economic thinking. It suggests that economic growth is driven by labor, not by investment, and that expenditures on human resource development are more than social overhead capital.

Living the Faith

While I still try my hand at theoretical and research matters from time to time in pursuit of the elusive holistic model of development, I mostly give myself completely to the task of coping with our imperfect world.

The substance of my work at the World Bank is to help improve the lot of existing societies wracked by poverty, disease, hunger, and ignorance. My work provides ample scope to live the faith on a daily basis. Rationalist ethics take command when I let conscience guide the myriad decisions that come my way. The dictates of living the faith transcend sound, conscientious professionalism, important as that may be, and lead me to try to promote the justly balanced society both within the World Bank community and within the countries we serve. Happily, the World Bank is an ideal place for a person of conscience to work. It is institutionally committed to the lofty ideals of promoting economic growth and poverty alleviation throughout the world. It is open to thoughtful and rational debate on how best to pursue these goals. New ideas are thrashed out with considerable objectivity.

The Bank has already crossed the political bridge of deciding where it stands. The debates of the early 1970s on "redistribution with growth" buried the notion that income distribution was a subject beyond the scope of international agencies or that it concerned only the domestic politics of sovereign states.

Within the Bank, living the faith means several things. It means the pursuit of truth. Evidence must be carefully scrutinized and close attention paid to what is really happening as projects are implemented. Research must be promoted on complex issues, and the mind kept open to the best possible solutions. Truth is approached by asking, probing, and seeking knowledge.

Living the faith means speaking the truth. "Embarrassing" issues cannot be glossed over; "delicate" matters cannot be excluded. Commitment to truth must include the will to stand up and be counted on important issues, however controversial they may be.

Living the faith also means acting on the truth, as God gives us to understand the truth. Analysis and discussion must be followed by concrete actions. Policies, programs, and projects that can be supported technically and financially by the international community must be promoted. Reformers within the governments of developing countries must be supported, and the international community mobilized to support worthy reform endeavors.

Living the faith means giving voice to the disenfranchised in the world — the millions of small farmers and poor urban dwellers whose political weakness is often a cause of their unending misery. It means recognizing issues of gender inequities and siding with the vulnerable in society in their time of need. Their interests need to be represented in the corridors of power where key policies and decisions are debated.

Living the faith means balancing the interests of alternative claimants in a just and equitable manner, not solely on a technical and legalistic basis. The need for justice and equity is particularly urgent and relevant in the case of the present debt crisis, in which competing, valid claims to limited resources require constant arbitration. The sanctity of contracts, the taxation of those already overburdened, the requirements of international trade, justice and equity in burden sharing — all are ingredients in what must remain one of the more difficult problems to negotiate. Finding the appropriate formula depends on the specific circumstances, but two aspects most important in these complex and technical negotiations are: 1) a clear understanding of who is paying for what, and 2) a balanced approach to matching realistic claims to ability to pay.

Living the faith also means promoting international cooperation. This can involve promoting better dialogue between developed and developing countries, working toward balanced terms of trade, or promoting international transactions. It also means promoting regional integration, which is both an increasingly inescapable economic necessity, and an eminently desirable socio-political objective. Sub-Saharan Africa offers a real challenge to take seriously the call to universalism: regional institution-building efforts must be grappled with in the face of nationalism and in spite of a long history of strife and failed attempts.

The pursuit of a justly balanced society in a world battered by poverty and bereft of equity is a challenging task. Poverty alleviation and attention to basic needs are not "add-ons" to our basic task of promoting economic growth. They are central to development and give meaning and substance to the efforts we engage in day in, day out. Alternating between stridency and quiet persuasion, I have been determined in preaching and practicing the art of designing national economic adjustment programs that make the social dimensions of those programs a central component of the decision-making process.

As stewards of the earth, how can we remain silent in the face of continuing environmental degradation, especially in Africa? The frightful toll of desertification and deforestation is creating a nightmarish reality where green and lush landscapes once existed. Recent numbers show that Africa's 703 million hectares of undisturbed forest in 1980 were being cleared at the rate of 3.7 million hectares per year, even as 55 million Africans face acute scarcity of fuel wood. Moreover, 80 to 90 percent of rangelands, 80 percent of rain-fed croplands, and 30 percent of irrigated lands are affected by desertification.

Promoting an aggressive campaign to reverse these trends and restore the natural environment is not just a mission of mercy to a particularly stricken land, but an essential part of our role here on this earth: to take care of it and pass it on, enriched but unsullied, to a generation yet unborn.

Outside of the World Bank, I pursue a parallel set of interests in promoting cultural authenticity in the contemporary artistic expression of Muslim societies. My chosen field is architecture and architectural criticism, for architecture is the physical mirror of a society, reflecting its weaknesses and ills just as much as its serenity and its well being. Without romanticizing the past, the superb "fit" of vernacular architecture in poor societies such as Mali or Niger clearly reflects the serenity of a well established cultural order that can remain at peace with itself in spite of severe hardship.[3] By contrast, how much do the "modern" cities of the third world speak of "angst" and the "zeitgeist"! Their throbbing energy is companion to abject misery and a confused image of self and society.

Against this degrading poverty and this loss of identity, the architectural critic becomes a constructive, creative force. The critic can and should speak the truth as he or she sees it, and help promote a balance between respect for the past and the needs of the present, reminding people to remain true to themselves and their own identity. The concept of stewardship of the earth deals with the relationship between human beings and their environment, both natural and man-made.

These two aspects of my work come together to round out my professional life as do the Yin and the Yang. One without the other would be less than fully satisfying. It is both my good fortune and my joy to live and work in a place that enables me to give full scope to these interests.

* * *

The authors of this volume are in agreement about the great issues of the day: strident nationalism; war and its most sinister form, nuclear holocaust; the absence of ethical beliefs which allows rampant consumerism and runaway military budgets to coexist with degrading poverty, malnutrition, and hunger; the absence of respect for fundamental human rights; the degradation of our environment in pursuit of short term profits; and the absence of a holistic view to deal with these problems.

The path to dealing with the issues that beset the world

is for each individual and each group to start to reform itself. There has been all too much emphasis placed on reforming the other person, the other nation. Let each person base his or her conduct on principles firmly rooted in our own ethical traditions. Let us each try to live up to our own lofty standards.

NOTES

1. Robert S. McNamara, *Address to the Board of Governors,* The World Bank, Washington, D.C., Sept. 26, 1977, p. 7.
2. For example, see Stephen Jay Gould, *The Mismeasure of Man.* New York: W.W. Norton, 1982, p. 74.
3. For a discussion of the effects of accelerated modernization on such an environment, see I. Serageldin, "Rural Architecture In the Yemen Arab Republic." In *The Changing Rural Habitat,* Volume I: Case Studies, pp. 1–10. Proceedings of Seminar Six in the Series Architectural Transformations in the Islamic World, held in Beijing, People's Republic of China, October 19–22, 1981. Singapore: Concept Media Pte Ltd., for the Aga Khan Award for Architecture, 1982.

Afterword

David Beckmann

Each of the essays in this book is a confession of faith and an explanation of the relationship of our faith to the roles we play in the world and in economic development. All of us agree that humanity is headed toward very serious difficulties — possibly catastrophic — unless spiritual values come to have more influence on the course of human development. Though recent events in Eastern Europe are encouraging, we believe that the general neglect of ethical and religious considerations is perilous for the modern world.

We did not begin our discussions together with a conviction of impending disaster. None of us is by disposition a pessimist, and we would really rather not hold this alarming point of view. But as we have articulated our beliefs and their implications, our traditions and our analyses of current realities have pushed us to it. Beckmann and Serageldin would say that we stand under the judgment of God. Agarwala and Burmester would say that we stand at a crossroads in human evolution. But we all believe that the current course of world history must be reshaped by ethics to avert disastrous consequences.

In our time, more than ever before, the whole world lives one history. All religious and ethical traditions must respond to the shared global experience of the twentieth century. For all of us, certain political and economic problems have, perforce, taken on religious importance. Over the past generation, humanity has developed the capacity to extinguish itself through nuclear weaponry. This new reality gives all history a more somber tone, especially since our century is also characterized by unprecedented nationalism. The Cold War has thawed, but the Middle East is engulfed in war, and world military expenditure has not declined much. Turmoil in the Soviet Union suggests new scenarios that might trigger nuclear war.

Since the world has become much more thoroughly linked together through electronic communications and economic commerce, the traditional quest for social justice is now necessarily global in scope. In a world where we see victims of famine on the nightly news, we cannot limit compassion to people in our own country. In a world where nearly a fifth of everything produced is traded across national borders, every ethical tradition urges us to reduce the abject, hungry poverty that persists in large parts of the world. Nor can we pretend that the brutal suppression of human rights that still persists throughout much of the world is none of our business.

It is also clear that the unprecedented economic growth of the last generation has strained the natural environment — in some ways, past the breaking point. To protect the environment that sustains us, will it be necessary to drastically reduce standards of living in the industrial countries? Or will it be possible to maintain economic growth, but change the pattern of growth in ways that reduce environmental cost (by cutting back further on the use of fossil fuels, for example)?

We do not agree among ourselves about how radical a change environmental constraints will require. But no ethical tradition could be unmoved by the prospect of permanently damaging the earth that sustains us. Protecting the planet will definitely require far-reaching change, especially in the industrial countries.

The four authors of this book are, on balance, positively impressed by the record and future potential of modern scientific and economic progress. Burmester is most heavily influenced by science, but all of us are intent that faith be open to experimental truth and not insulated from science by unthinking dogma. We judge that the rapid economic development of the last two hundred years — and the accelerated worldwide development of the last generation — have resulted in much more good than evil. But material progress has brought unprecedented power for evil, too. Humanity's various ethical traditions all teach a basically common morality — values such as honesty, humility, and concern for others. But materialism and secularism have weakened people's will actually to do what they believe is right.

Because of the risk of nuclear war, the explosiveness of injustice in an interdependent world, and the possibilities for environmental destruction, the world needs morally motivated people more than ever before. Yet modern life often seems devoid of any purpose more powerful than achieving affluence.

The authors diagnose the spiritual malaise somewhat differently and prescribe different remedies. Agarwala thinks the root problem is the mistaken modern myth that evolution and progress come about through conflict. He prescribes a new integration of science and religion. Biology and what he calls "science of the spirit" would both be built on the notion that evolution is the gradual revelation of the divine potential in all things.

Beckmann says the root of the problem is a lack of moral energy, and he hopes that the widespread discussion of world problems, citizen activism, and Christian revitalization may stir up additional energy for the tasks at hand.

Burmester emphasizes people's sense of purposelessness, especially in countries where people do not have to worry much about meeting their material needs. He suggests a new paradigm that would give meaning to life. It would focus on the task of meeting basic needs globally, a resurgence of individualism, and new creative endeavors. Serageldin suggests that the root problem may be the inadequacy of contemporary creeds, especially the narrow creed of nationalism. He says we should all begin by reforming ourselves: Muslims would reform their societies in keeping with God's charge that man be his viceregent and the steward of creation.

These diagnoses of humanity's problem are grounded in our various traditions. Because Beckmann and Serageldin both worship the God of Abraham, they expect to find spiritual vitality in God's grace and in new obedience. Beckmann, true to his Christian faith, stresses the vitalizing power of God's grace, while Serageldin, true to his Muslim faith, stresses human action.

Burmester and Agarwala scan general human experience — not any special revelation — for spiritual guidance, and both think of human destiny primarily in terms of human evolution. They are less concerned than Beckmann and Serageldin about being loyal to any particular tradition. Yet Burmester, true to his Western roots, tends to think of evolution moving forward through spurts of human creativity (a Buddha or Jesus, a Bach or Einstein), while Agarwala, true to his Hindu roots, looks for evolution to move forward through the integration of diverse truths and peoples.

Although our delineation of the world's great problems is similar, these divergences of spiritual analysis lead us to emphasize different kinds of global reform. Agarwala stresses ways of integrating science and religion and of drawing the world's peoples together through new international institutions, markets that function well, and a Gandhi-like movement of simple living and charity. Beckmann hopes for a revival of flagging spirits to motivate more and better efforts at disarmament and economic development. Such efforts would be intensified and reformed, but would be basically along the lines of liberal reform over the last generation.

Burmester is more daring about what moral efforts might achieve, and so he challenges us to aim for radical changes: dramatically decreasing armaments, population, and resource consumption. Serageldin calls for each to reform himself, and accordingly he concentrates his attention on what "stewardship" implies for Muslims and on the model of a "justly balanced society" for Muslim countries.

These various paths of action can be complementary. But Agarwala and Burmester think Beckmann's faith in Jesus Christ and Serageldin's faith in the Quran are remnants from a more primitive era, no longer viable in the modern world. Beckmann and Serageldin, on the other hand, find the faith of Agarwala and Burmester in the moral inclinations of humanity to be unrealistic and misleading.

But we all have religious reasons for hope. Agarwala believes that the divine potential in humanity will indeed win out. Burmester thinks, although he is not quite sure, that people will reform if they understand it to be in their own interest. Serageldin hopes that reason and revelation will inspire individuals and nations to right action. Beckmann's hope is that God will be patient with humanity, as he has so often been in the past.

Our pilgrimage together, on Friday mornings and in writing this book, has helped us confront the complex business of bringing spiritual values to bear on secular affairs. In closing, we would call attention to the process that gave rise to this book — listening to people from other nations and cultures. As the world has become smaller and more vulnerable, dialogue among its people has become a matter of life or death.

The World Bank is itself an instrument of international understanding. Every Tuesday morning the Bank's board of directors meets. It represents 154 nations and, thus, tremendous political and cultural diversity. There are sometimes sharp debates in the Bank's board. Yet with surprisingly little fanfare or rancor, they every year approve some $20 billion in projects to promote growth and reduce poverty in the developing countries.

This is possible, partly because discussion in the Bank is focused on pragmatic measures to foster economic and social development. The directors do not give speeches to each other on such broad issues as the threat of a nuclear war. A director would seldom use the board to air a political dispute between one nation and another. Religious and cultural differences go unspoken. Having set to one side so many potentially divisive issues, the board can usually reach consensus on measures to raise the income of small-scale farmers or to help a country use its energy resources more effectively. Sometimes the directors can agree on cooperative steps to address contentious issues such as international debt or deforestation in developing countries. One member of the Friday group calls the Bank's board meetings the "Tuesday morning miracle."

International institutions such as the World Bank are a relatively new, still limited, but precious phenomenon in human history. The Bank's Friday group represents something even newer, indeed embryonic — the deepening, increasingly intimate interconnectedness of the world's peoples. Our meetings are small, allowing for rich interpersonal relations. Our conversation ranges from the economic and technical aspects of development, to global trends and issues, to cultural, moral, and spiritual questions. We delve into political and religious issues that could be profoundly divisive.

Yet we have found that such discussion need not be divisive at all. On the contrary, it has brought us closer together, and given us new clarity and energy for the nitty-gritty tasks of our work in global development.